Haldane's Best Employment Websites For Professionals

Bernard Haldane Associates

IMPACT PUBLICATIONS
Manassas Park, VA

Library of Congress Cataloguing-in-Publication Data

Bernard Haldane Associates
    Haldane's best employment websites for professionals / Bernard Haldane Associates
        p. cm. – (Haldane's best series; 5)
    Includes bibliographical references and index.
    ISBN 1-57023-176-1
    1. Job hunting – Computer network resources – Handbooks, manuals, etc.
2. Job hunting – Information services – Computer network resources – Handbooks, manuals, etc. 3. Professions – Vocational guidance – Computer network resources – Handbooks, manuals, etc. 4. Professions – Information services – Computer network resources – Handbooks, manuals, etc. 5. Internet searching – Handbooks, manuals, etc. 6. Internet – Handbooks, manuals, etc. 7. World Wide Web – Handbooks, manuals, etc. 8. Web sites – Directories. I. Title: Employment websites for professionals. II. Bernard Haldane Associates. III. Series.

HF5382.7 .H3292001   2001039901
025.06'65014–dc21

Publisher: For information on Impact Publications, including current and forthcoming publications, authors, press kits, online bookstore, and submission requirements, visit our website: www.impactpublications.com.

Publicity/Rights: For information on publicity, author interviews, and subsidiary rights, contact the Media Relations Department: Tel. 703-361-7300, Fax 703-335-9486, or email: info@impactpublications.com.

Sales/Distribution: All bookstore sales are handled through Impact's trade distributor: National Book Network, 15200 NBN Way, Blue Ridge Summit, PA 17214, Tel. 1-800-462-6420. All other sales and distribution inquiries should be directed to the publisher: Sales Department, IMPACT PUBLICATIONS, 9104 Manassas Drive, Suite N, Manassas Park, VA 20111-5211, Tel. 703-361-7300, Fax 703-335-9486, or email: info@impactpublications.com.

Haldane's Best Employment Websites For Professionals

Books in Haldane's Best Series

Contents

Don't Just Change Your Job. Change Your Life™
A Personal Invitation

Jerold Weinger
Chairman of the Board and CEO
Bernard Haldane Associates

I AM PLEASED YOU ARE JOINING US ON WHAT MAY WELL become one of the most exciting journeys, and defining moments, in your career and your life – finding the right job that truly reflects what you do well and enjoy doing. This journey could change your life in many positive ways.

Let us talk truth about finding jobs: most anyone can find a job without a great deal of wisdom or effort. So why do you need a job search book or a career professional? Because only a few people know how to find the perfect job – one they really love doing and going to each day. Finding the right job takes time and effort as well as special expertise. Indeed, finding a job is often a frustrating and humbling experience of marketing one's skills, experience, and accomplishments to unenlightened strangers. It requires doing first things first – identifying your unique talents, formulating a clear objective, and organizing a step-by-step job search that puts you in the right place, with the right people, at the right time. Above all, it requires conducting a smart employer-centered job search that incorporates appropriate use of the Internet at every stage of one's job search. And that is one of many things we do well at Bernard Haldane Associates. It is something I want to share with you, regardless of whether or not you become one of our clients. I want you to discover the joys of finding your perfect "fit" in today's job market.

I am pleased you have chosen this particular book, which represents the fifth volume in the ***Haldane's Best Series***. I am especially pleased because I believe you will benefit tremendously from our job search and career management approach as it relates to the Internet. We do not just write books and give advice. As a leading career management organization, we have over 50 years of experience working in the job search trenches with a wide range of clients. Best of all, we have a solid track record of success in helping clients find exciting jobs that also advance their careers. We empower them with sound career management tools, including the latest online resources for conducting an effective job search.

> *Skilled in using search engines, email, and specific employment sites, our clients learn how to harness the power of the Internet to conduct a Haldane-principled job search.*

Our approach to managing an effective job search has worked well for hundreds of thousands of clients as well as millions of others who have benefitted indirectly from our career management principles. As recruitment and the job search have increasingly moved to the Internet, so have our job-finding strategies and techniques. Indeed, we embrace the Internet because, if used appropriately, it enables job seekers to use a powerful information tool to enhance their job search. Skilled in using search engines, email, and specific employment sites, our clients learn how to harness the power of the Internet to conduct a Haldane-principled job search.

That is exactly what we want you to do in using this book – incorporate the best of the Internet in your job search rather than conduct an Internet job search. This is an important distinction that will quickly become apparent in the following pages. We purposefully organized this book around key steps in the job search process rather than creating a directory of so-called "best websites."

As we note in the following chapters, the Internet is a very seductive medium which, if you are not careful, can lead you down the wrong job search path. In fact, many employment websites, which are primarily recruitment sites, promote a much flawed job search approach. Don't be seduced too soon. Do first things first, which is not to write a resume or go online to browse job listings and prematurely enter your resume into an online database. Rather, organize a job search that incorporates a few useful websites for enhancing each stage of your job search.

Like other books in the *Haldane's Best Series*, this is not your typical job search book. It represents the collective efforts of Haldane career professionals who have assisted hundreds of thousands of clients during the past 50+ years in finding jobs and advancing careers. Experienced in the day-to-day realities of finding jobs and changing careers, our work continues to represent the cutting edge of career management. Indeed, we have pioneered many innovative assessment, networking, interviewing, and salary negotiating techniques that are now standard practices among career professionals and job seekers. Our proprietary CS2K program harnesses the power of the Internet in conducting an effective job search. While this program is only available to our clients, this book will give you a glimpse into how clients use the Internet as well as conduct an effective job search. If you follow the advice outlined in this book, you should take charge of your job search via the Internet. You'll begin using online resources for developing a powerful Haldane-principled job search.

I also invite you to contact our offices in the United States, Canada, and the United Kingdom. Consisting of a network of more than 90 career management offices, Bernard Haldane Associates works with thousands of clients each day in conducting effective job searches based upon the many principles outlined in the *Haldane's Best Series*. In the Appendix, as well as on our website, we include contact information on the offices nearest you:

<u>www.jobhunting.com</u>

Please join us as we celebrate more than a half century of helping hundreds of thousands of professionals realize their career dreams. Do what we advise our clients to do each day – incorporate the best of the Internet into a smart job search where wisdom guides the selection and use of websites in one's job search.

Haldane's Best Employment Websites For Professionals

1

A Web of Career Opportunities

FINDING A JOB IN TODAY'S HIGHLY COMPETITIVE JOB market requires the efficient and effective communication of qualifications to employers. Since employers and recruiters need to cost-effectively locate and screen talent, many aspects of the traditional hiring process have become automated through the use of sophisticated HR software and recruitment websites.

Only a few years ago, most job searches were conducted primarily via the telephone, mail, fax, and face-to-face meetings because of the traditional structure of recruitment. Not so today. More and more recruitment takes place in Internet time. Not surprising, individuals with Internet job search skills increasingly have a competitive edge with employers and recruiters in today's new digital job market.

Internet Time For Everyone

Finding a job increasingly requires incorporating the Internet into one's job search because employers are cost-effectively organizing recruitment around this powerful communication medium. Indeed, several companies, such as Dow Chemical, no longer accept mailed resumes and cold calls. Instead, they require that all inquiries, resume submissions, and applications be done via their company website. Send a nicely crafted traditional resume and letter by mail or fax and it may be returned to you with a note instructing you on how to properly communicate your interests to the company – direct your inquiry to the company website!

> *If you've not incorporated the Internet into your job search, it's time you do so before the train passes you by or confines you to the end of the line.*

If you are not incorporated the Internet into your job search, it is time you do so before the train passes you by or confines you to the end of the line. That's our purpose in writing this book – to quickly get you up and running with a well organized and targeted job search, preferably based on Haldane's career management principles, that is closely linked to the use of key employment-related sites on the Internet as outlined in this book.

Different Needs, Benefits, and Skills

The Internet has added many new dimensions to the job search just within the past few years. For job seekers, the Internet plays important roles in four key phases of the job search – conducting research, networking for information and advice, submitting resumes and online applications, and communicating with employers, recruiters, and others. Job seekers increasingly need to develop and refine three key Internet skills which involve the use of:

1. Search engines and directories for conducting research on jobs, employers, and the job market.

2. Usenet newsgroups, mailing lists, and community forums or message boards of websites for acquiring data and networking for information, advice, and referrals.

3. Email for sending resumes, letters, applications, and other forms of communication as well as for receiving messages.

In fact, savvy job seekers who frequently use the Internet essentially perfect these two online skills:

1. Use search engines, agents, and directories.

2. Manage email, both outgoing and incoming.

If you learn these two skills well, you should be in excellent shape to incorporate the best of the Internet into your job search. You will be more than just Internet-savvy – you'll be a savvy job seeker who organizes a powerful job search around Haldane's principles for conducting a combined online and offline job search. Best of all, you will be on the cutting edge of today's digital job market.

Check Your Internet Job I.Q.

No mistake about it – it's a jungle out there when conducting a job search. What initially seems simple – conducting a job search – has a tendency to become very complex and challenging. High expectations of landing a great new job often give way to the day-to-day realities of trying to get strangers to take you and your career seriously by inviting you to job interviews. You have to sell yourself to lots of people. It's an especially messy jungle if you lack focus and don't have a good job search plan and some basic information on what to do and where to go both inside and outside cyberspace.

While you may be a very competent Internet user when dealing with other aspects of your personal and professional lives, just how savvy are you when it comes to using the Internet to deal with one of the most important decisions of your life – changing jobs or careers? Do you know how to organize an effective job search that integrates the Internet into the whole job finding process? Can you accelerate your job search efforts by using key websites? Do you know which websites will give you the biggest bang for your online efforts? Let's start by responding to the following statements. Indicate your degree of agreement (5) and disagreement (1) to each statement:

	Agree				Disagree

1. I consider myself a very Internet savvy person, from finding information and organizing files to handling email.   5 4 3 2 1

2. I know how to organize and implement an effective job search with or without the Internet.   5 4 3 2 1

3. I'm acquainted with the Haldane approach to conducting a job search.   5 4 3 2 1

4. I regularly receive and transmit email.   5 4 3 2 1

5. I know how to handle email attachments.   5 4 3 2 1

6. I know when it is and is not appropriate to use email in my job search.   5 4 3 2 1

7. I have an Internet resume which I can send to employers and recruiters as well as upload to employment websites.   5 4 3 2 1

8. I know how to properly send my resume by email.   5 4 3 2 1

9. I regularly use email for follow-up purposes.   5 4 3 2 1

10. I know the pros and cons of blasting my resume by email to thousands of employers and recruiters.   5 4 3 2 1

11. I know how to measure the effectiveness of employment websites.   5 4 3 2 1

12. I know how employers use websites for recruitment purposes.   5 4 3 2 1

13. I know which five search engines produce the best search results.   5 4 3 2 1

14. I can find online directories of the major employment websites.   5 4 3 2 1

15. I know how to join newsgroups
as well as develop my own mailing list. 5 4 3 2 1

16. I can locate at least five professional
associations on the Internet related to
my career field. 5 4 3 2 1

17. I save time looking for job boards by
using at least two gateway websites. 5 4 3 2 1

18. I know which mega employment websites
include the most job postings. 5 4 3 2 1

19. I know which mega employment websites
include specialized job search services
related to my career interests. 5 4 3 2 1

20. I have a well organized job search plan
that is tied to several useful websites. 5 4 3 2 1

21. I know at least 20 different free job search
services I can acquire over the Internet. 5 4 3 2 1

22. I spend 20-30% of my job search time
on the Internet. 5 4 3 2 1

23. I can find at least five websites for
conducting online self-assessments. 5 4 3 2 1

24. I know where to find online education
programs and courses for improving my
skills and professional development. 5 4 3 2 1

25. I can quickly find information on
employers by accessing at least three
major gateway business research sites. 5 4 3 2 1

26. I know where to get online career
advice from the experts. 5 4 3 2 1

27. If I need assistance in writing my resume
and letters, I know which websites can
provide me with appropriate expertise. 5 4 3 2 1

28. I know which websites will get my resume
into the hands of thousands of recruiters. 5 4 3 2 1

29. I know the best five websites that
    provide executive-level job search services.   5 4 3 2 1

30. I can quickly find my old school and/or
    military buddies by using several websites.   5 4 3 2 1

31. I know which three websites will quickly
    give me information on salary comparables.   5 4 3 2 1

32. I know where to find a professional career
    counselor online.   5 4 3 2 1

33. I can find at least 10 websites that focus
    solely on my occupational specialty.   5 4 3 2 1

34. I know the websites of the major staffing
    and recruiting firms.   5 4 3 2 1

35. I can quickly find key relocation
    information on other communities.   5 4 3 2 1

TOTAL   _____

When finished responding to each statement, add up your answers
to get an overall composite score. If your score is 150 or higher, you
have a very high Internet Job I.Q. Indeed, this book will help you fine-
tune how you have already linked the Internet to your well organized
job search. If your score is below 125, you'll find most of the following
chapters to be of considerable help in organizing your job search with
the use of the Internet. If your score is below 100, we have a lot of
work to do to make sure you are conducting an Internet-savvy job
search. You should find our information and recommendations to be
especially enlightening for both organizing your job search and using
key Internet sites at each stage of your job search.

Once you finish this book, consider responding again to each item
in this exercise. Chances are you will now be conducting a well organized job search that is closely integrated with many key websites we've
outlined. Best of all, you'll be on the road to conducting a Haldane-
based campaign that has proven very effective for hundreds of thousands of Bernard Haldane Associates' clients.

Using the Internet With Caution and Wisdom

The Internet is both a boon and bane to job seekers. On the one hand, it offers a wealth of employment information and services that theoretically should make one's job search efforts quick and easy. Just go to Monster.com, HotJobs.com, Careerbuilder.com, or Headhunter.net, and thousands of employers and job listings, as well as numerous peripheral job search services, unfold before your eyes. And that's just the beginning of the many employment riches found in cyberspace. It's like one big beautiful flower garden where almost everything for job seekers is free for the picking.

On the other hand, what you think you see on the Internet is not always what you get. Like the Internet medium in general, employment websites are often overwhelming, over-hyped, and deceptive. Privacy also is becoming a major issue with some sites that may resell your personal online information. By some estimates, over 100,000 employment-related websites currently operate on the Internet. In some cases, a fancy website may have 300 employees working in a digital sweatshop to keep it well and alive. At the same time, another equally attractive website may be operated by two part-time entrepreneurs from their bedrooms at night. Identifying and navigating through only a fraction of these sites can be a daunting task. Yes, indeed, it's a real jungle if you don't know the "what" and "where" of this elusive but always fascinating medium that appears kind to job seekers but is primarily financed by employers in search of cost-effective talent.

Our task in the following chapters is to help you make better sense, as well as use good judgment, in using this medium to find a job. Like a Career Advisor, we are here to help you identify and use the best websites for employment purposes. Most important of all, we examine numerous employment-related websites from two important "qualifying" perspectives:

1. Websites of particular interest to professionals – those making in excess of $40,000 a year.

2. Websites that are compatible with our notion of what constitutes an effective job search for you, the job seeker.

As such, we are picky, as well as critical, about what we choose to include and exclude in this book and what we have to say when evaluating the efficacy of individual sites for job seekers. We are especially critical of many mega employment websites that are primarily designed as huge classified ad operations – include thousands of job listings for job seekers to browse and thousands of resumes in a database for employers to browse. Not surprising, these often attractive and tempting "job board" sites promote a much flawed job search approach, which you are well advised to approach with caution. They are designed in the interests of their paying customers – employers – to generate as many resumes as possible in response to job vacancies. If you primarily use these sites in your job search, you will be trying to find a job you can fit into rather than one that is fit for you – just like responding to classified ads in newspapers.

Employer-Centered Websites

Most employment-oriented websites are designed to meet the needs of employers and recruiters who need to recruit talent. They are not designed to help job seekers find their perfect jobs. Only a handful of websites are structured in the best interests of job seekers. After all, the economics of the Web are such that employers and recruiters financially support these websites; job seekers can use most of these websites free of charge. From the perspective of employers and recruiters, these are first and foremost **recruitment websites**. Since they pay for the privilege of posting job vacancies, searching for resumes, and advertising their company through banner and button ads, these websites are employer-centered. From the perspective of job seekers, these are free **job search sites** where individuals can post their resumes, browse job postings, and acquire useful job search information. Such sites encourage job seekers to conduct a resume-centered job search – your resume in response to job listings – rather than an accomplishment- and motivation-based job search.

As you cut through much of the clutter and noise on the Internet, you will find thousands of employment websites that beg for attention. As we will see in subsequent chapters, most employment-related sites are structured around a traditional advertising model – employers pay for ads, job postings, and access to the online resume database.

Our job is to assist you in using these and other websites to your advantage. Rather than focusing solely on employer-centered websites which operate like huge classified ad publications, you should seek out and regularly use websites that will enhance each step of your job search. In other words, we need to shift the focus from employer-centered websites to job seeker-centered websites. Rather than passively entering your resume online and browsing job postings, you should be proactive in finding websites that will enable you to assess skills, clarify your objective, acquire employment information, network for information and advice, write and distribute your resume, and prepare you for the job interview and salary negotiations.

An Internet Job Search?

We have purposefully avoided talking about conducting an "Internet job search" because such terminology is somewhat misleading. It could easily distract you from what should be your central focus – conducting an effective job search. Unfortunately, many people mistake the medium for the message – the Internet becomes equated with the job search. They spend an inordinate amount of time behind a computer screen trying to conduct a job search because they believe one of today's great job hunting myths – jobs are primarily found using the Internet. Nothing could be further from the truth. The Internet is a wonderful resource for acquiring information and communicating with others. As you will quickly discover, most employment-related websites are basically recruitment websites for employers who wish to cost-effectively screen candidates for interviews by acquiring resumes from a large pool of qualified job seekers. They are not job search sites designed with your (the candidate's) best job search interests in mind – finding a job that is a perfect "fit" for your particular mix of interests, motivations, skills, and abilities. If they were structured in this manner, they would not be free to the end-user. Indeed, you would pay dearly for such special job seeker-centered services which are usually associated with testing centers, and other career professionals. Most employment websites remain free to job seekers because they essentially "belong" to employers who control the outcomes.

Whatever you do, avoid the temptation to conduct an Internet job search. Use the Internet as part of your job search but don't let it consume all of your time. If you do, it can quickly take you down a traditional job finding path which will not be in your best interests – responding to job postings and entering your resume into electronic databases. A good rule of thumb to follow is to spend no more than 20 percent of your job search time using the Internet and focus most of this time on research and networking activities. After all, surveys show that less that five percent of job seekers find jobs through the Internet. The other 80 percent of your time should be spent on non-Internet-related activities that advance your job search toward the goal of finding a job you do well and enjoy doing. You do this by using the telephone and meeting with people face-to-face to exchange information, advice, and referrals. You should focus on networking and getting interviews rather than only surveying and responding to job listings and submitting applications.

Job Searching With the Web

Make sure you use the Internet wisely in your job search by integrating it into each step of your job search. While most websites primarily focus on the resume writing and application steps of a job search, your job search should include the Internet in this sequence of steps and activities:

1. Self-assessment
2. Goal-setting
3. Researching jobs and employers
4. Writing resumes and letters
5. Networking for information, advice, and referrals
6. Applying for jobs
7. Interviewing for jobs
8. Negotiating salary and terms of employment

Since most employment-related websites are designed for employers and recruiters, they primarily focus on resumes (Step 4) and applications (Step 6). The secret to making the Internet work in your best interests is to incorporate it in all eight job search steps. That's why we focus on using the Internet to enhance a well organized and targeted job search rather than conducting an Internet job search. This is an important distinction which you should always remember when using the Internet, and especially if you become captivated by the richness of employment information and the multiplicity of employers encouraging you to contact them with your resume. As we do each day with our many clients, our goal is to assist you in using the Internet wisely for conducting an effective job search.

The Haldane Approach and Network

While the information in this book will help you use the Internet in your own job search, at the same time, you may want to take advantage of the Bernard Haldane Associates network of support services which consists of hundreds of career professionals, called Career Advisors, in more than 90 offices in the United States, Canada, and the United Kingdom (see the Appendix for a complete listing of this network of offices). Anyone can conduct a job search on their own and find a job. But we assume you don't want to find just any job. You want a high quality job that is the right "fit" for both you and the employer – one you really enjoy doing and one that benefits both you and the employer.

Unfortunately, the novice do-it-yourself approach often results in taking shortcuts rather than doing first things first. For example, most job seekers begin their job search by first writing their resume rather than doing the necessary foundation work that should be the basis for their resume and other key job search activities, such as networking, interviewing, and negotiating. The Internet further encourages this approach because of the presence of so many recruitment sites that are designed to persuade job seekers to focus on their resume – respond to job listings with a resume and enter your resume into the site's resume database. After all, many job seekers say, isn't that what you're supposed to do first – focus on writing and distributing your resume – because that's what others always do? Some, as indicated by the

> ### Client Feedback
>
> *"Right from the beginning, Haldane's techniques helped build my self esteem, gave me direction, and helped me increase my salary 100% more than my previous position with less frustration and stress than before."*
> **– M.H.**

popularity of resume example books, even creatively plagiarize others' resumes. By following the crowd, they literally put the horse before the cart and thereby immediately handicap their job search with an ill-fitting resume that may communicate all the wrong messages!

You owe it to yourself to present your very best self to employers. That means taking the time and spending some money to do first things first when conducting a job search. The prerequisite foundation work involves self-assessment and goal setting – two activities that may be best done with the assistance of a career professional. In Chapter 4, we'll give you a sampling of websites that offer testing and assessment services online. If you fail to do this foundation work and go directly to writing your resume and interviewing for jobs, you will most likely join thousands of other do-it-yourself job seekers who meander through the job market trying to find a job they can fit into. You will find a job but chances are it will not be a good fit. You may be well advised to work with a career professional to identify what it is you do well and enjoy doing.

> *Very few job seekers conduct this process well on their own. Not that they can't; it's just that they won't and thus they don't.*

The Haldane approach, which also is known as Success Factor Analysis, has helped hundreds of thousands of clients who use Haldane's career management services for coaching them through the job search process. With the assistance of a professional career coach who helps them with assessment, goal setting, resume writing, referral interviews, and job interviews, these individuals go on to find jobs that are excellent fits. While these same individuals could conduct a job search on their own, they choose to work with a professional who can assist them every step of the way. The professional does not find them a job. Instead, their career coach provides important career services, advice, and structure that enables the individual to become successful on his or her own terms. In the process, they acquire important long-term career development skills that will serve them well throughout their worklife.

Let's talk truth about what we're dealing with in the world of self-help and enlightenment. Despite the ostensibly friendly and job-rich

Internet, it can be very lonely and depressing out there in the job market. Our experience, as well as that of most career professionals, is that very few job seekers conduct this process well on their own. Not that they can't; it's just that they won't and thus they don't. Understanding, yes; action, some, but not enough sustained, purposeful action to make things happen the way they should. Most job seekers can cognitively understand what's involved in conducting a successful job search, but the actual process of putting it all together, finding time, implementing each step properly, remaining focused, and maintaining a high level of motivation and energy in the face of no responses or ego-wrenching rejections is something that is very difficult to do on one's own. Not surprisingly, people normally used to being effective all of a sudden feel ineffective when conducting their own job search. Nothing seems to work according to expectation, or perhaps expectations are either too high or are misplaced. Job seekers procrastinate, find excuses, get depressed, escape to the Internet, and give up in what is often a cycle of good intentions and dashed expectations with sustained action conspicuously absent. Indeed, very few people ever do it right on their own. Accordingly, most people can benefit tremendously by using the services of a career expert. Career management professionals can save you time, money, and headaches because they combine expertise with a structure for implementing a job search campaign. This expertise comes in many forms:

- testing and assessing
- developing and targeting a job search plan
- assisting with writing resumes and letters
- honing networking skills
- implementing an action plan
- coaching for job interviews and salary negotiations

Most important of all, a professional can serve as a mentor who helps you maintain your focus and motivation as well as provides a critical structure for routinely implementing each phase of your job search.

At the same time, you need to be cautious in using so-called professional career services. This is a big business fraught with snake-oil salesmen and varying levels of competence. Professional career services come in many different forms, from testing and assessment centers to full-blown career marketing operations. Some individuals and companies offer career services at an hourly rate while others charge a flat contract price. If you work with someone who charges by the hour, be sure to know exactly what you need. Otherwise, you may be putting together a piecemeal job search that will most likely produce less than desirable outcomes. We prefer a contract arrangement that covers the complete job finding process, from start to finish. This type of arrangement avoids the chaos and excuses attendant with piecemeal activities; it focuses on every element in a successful job search. Most important of all, it commits the individual to seeing the process through at each step and doing everything possible to ensure success. Individuals use their time efficiently, remain focused, and handle well the psychological ups and downs of finding a job. Without such a long-term commitment and structure to move through the process expeditiously, individuals tend to conduct a haphazard job search, experience lots of psychological downs, and short-change their future by conducting a relatively ineffective job search.

Unfortunately, some career operations also are fraudulent. They take your money in exchange for broken promises. The promises usually come in the form of finding you a job. Many of these firms promise to do all the work for you – write your resume, broadcast it to hundreds of employers, and schedule interviews. All you have to do is write a check for this service and then sit back for the phone to ring. While this may sound good, because it appears to be a quick and easy way to find a job, such an approach is antithetical to the more than 50 years of Haldane experience.

At Bernard Haldane Associates we believe in doing first things first and coaching job seekers to do their very best. You team up with an experienced Career Advisor who literally takes you step-by-step through the complete career planning and job search process, from assessment, goal setting, researching, and resume and letter writing to networking, interviewing, and negotiating compensation. Many of our clients also use Haldane's proprietary Career Strategy 2000 (CS2K) program with the assistance of a Career Advisor. Designed specifically for Haldane's clients and incorporating the Haldane career management approach, this rich and powerful integrated electronic program, which is regularly updated, uses the Internet for conducting research, networking, distributing resumes, and targeting employers. Empowering our clients to manage their own careers, we do not find jobs for clients. That's not what we do nor should we be doing. Instead, we help you find a job through a well structured process that uses the best online and offline resources. This is an important distinction often lost in the job search business. It's a distinction that is central to writing Haldane resumes and letters, conducting Haldane referral and job interviews, using a Haldane-directed Internet approach, and negotiating compensation packages the Haldane way.

Websites For Professionals

Only a few years ago most employment-related websites were primarily geared to individuals with high-tech skills. Employers and recruiters in their high-demand fields staked out the Internet as one of the most fertile recruitment arenas. While thousands of high-tech recruitment sites continue to operate on the Internet, thousands of other sites that appeal to a large range of jobs seekers – from contract laborers to CEOs – also operate on the Internet. Indeed, almost every conceivable type of job and occupational field, including cloak-and-dagger spies, can be found on the Internet.

If you are a professional making in excess of $100,000 a year, most general employment websites will not be of interest to you because they are most relevant to the $30,000 to $70,000 a year wage earner. However, several websites now specialize in executive-level candidates who expect to be earning near or over six-figure salaries. Unlike most other employment websites, which are free to job seekers, many of these specialized sites charge job seekers membership fees for access to their resume database and job listings and using resume blasting services. Most of these sites are disproportionately linked to executive recruiters or headhunters who automatically receive resumes posted to these sites. If you primarily want to conduct a job search via head-hunters rather than directly with employers, you'll especially want to check out the resume blasting sites in Chapter 7 and the recruiter sites in Chapter 12. Since Bernard Haldane Associates works with numerous executive-level clients, our proprietary CS2K system is especially geared toward assisting these individuals in targeting a job search involving both employers and recruiters. Indeed, this is one of our specialties which is not well developed on the Internet.

Beyond Resume Databases and Job Postings

The following pages are designed to help you organize and energize your job search with the assistance of the Internet. While we review many of the most popular employment websites, which essentially function as resume databases and job posting sites, we're especially concerned that you use the Internet at each step in your job search. Whatever you do, don't become seduced into thinking that your job search and the Internet are one and the same. If you do, you are probably spending too much time on the Internet surfing through job postings and entering, re-entering, and revising your resume for the Web's many resume databases.

This book is all about being a savvy job seeker who uses **wisdom** to organize an effective job search and then link it to the Internet. If you organize your job search around Haldane principles, as outlined in our previous books, and then wed the Internet to your well-focused job search, you'll discover the power of the Internet more so than most other job seekers who conduct an Internet job search, which is basically a random search for jobs on the Internet.

If this is your first "Haldane's Best" volume, we urge you to also review our previous volumes (see the order form at the end of this book), which outline the Haldane career management approach:

Haldane's Best Resumes For Professionals
Haldane's Best Cover Letters For Professionals
Haldane's Best Answers to Tough Interview Questions
Haldane's Best Salary Tips For Professionals

Taken together, these books represent one of the most comprehensive libraries of career management theory and practice that has changed the lives of hundreds of thousands of people. We're pleased you are joining us on what has been our passion for over five decades – helping others find their passion in life. For more information on Bernard Haldane Associates, please visit our two websites as well as contact any of the offices listed in the Appendix of this book:

www.jobhunting.com

2

Organizing an Effective Job Search

FOR MORE THAN FIVE DECADES, BERNARD HALDANE Associates has pioneered many of the job search methods that are widely used by career professionals and job seekers around the world. These methods are based on a very simple yet compelling idea – you should find a job you do well and enjoy doing.

A Process, a Structure, and a Coach

Through a very well defined process, and with the assistance of a professional Career Advisor, our clients organize and implement a job search that is designed to connect them with a job that is a perfect "fit" for their particular interests, skills, and motivational pattern. Their success in landing the right job is a direct function of working with a Haldane Career Advisor who provides the necessary structure for organizing and implementing an effective job search. As coaches and facilitators, as well as experts in using Haldane's Web-based CS2K system, our Career Advisors assist clients in using the Internet at different stages of their job search, with special emphasis on conducting online research and managing contacts. Consistent with the Haldane career management approach, our Internet approach focuses on the needs of the job seeker (the job search) rather than on the needs of employers and recruiters (recruitment).

Unfortunately, most people do not know how to organize an effective job search. This is especially evident when you observe individuals using the Internet to find a job. They often begin by writing their resume and responding to job listings without first knowing what they do well and enjoy doing. Few can articulate a clear career objective – an employer-centered statement of what they hope to accomplish in the future. Trying to fit into a job rather than find a job that is fit for them, the typical job seeker wanders aimlessly in the job market in search of a job that may or may not be a good fit. Their notion of conducting a proactive job search campaign is to send out lots of resumes in response to job listings in the hope of getting a job interview.

> *Consistent with the Haldane career management approach, our Internet approach focuses on the needs of the job seeker rather than the needs of employers and recruiters.*

At the same time, many people can benefit from the assistance of a Career Advisor. At Bernard Haldane Associates our clients work one-on-one with such a career professional who assists them at every stage of their job search. A Career Advisor helps provide support, advice, and structure for conducting an effective job search.

Discover Your Best Self

Whatever you do, don't start your job search with a resume, unless you have done all the necessary preliminary work that resulted in creating a first-class resume reflecting the real you. Since your resume is your calling card for opening the doors of potential employers, it should first and foremost reflect who you really are and what you have done, can do, and will do in the future for an employer. Focusing on your goals, skills, and accomplishments, your resume should communicate your major strengths to employers. But before you can present yourself in a succinct one- to two-page resume, you need to become better acquainted with yourself – identify your very best self through a self-assessment process.

At Bernard Haldane Associates we recognize the power of self-assessment for organizing and guiding an effective job search. Self-assessment is the very first step in the process of managing one's career. Accordingly, our clients undergo different types of self-assessment in order to identify their *strengths* – those things they do well and enjoy doing – and their *pattern of accomplishments*. They discover through self-assessment their pattern of accomplishments which is the single most important piece of information employers need to know about their back-ground. This pattern includes their skills, motivations, and past accomplishments which come together as a predictable pattern of future performance. Since employers want to hire your future rather than your past, you need to clearly communicate to them your pattern of accomplishments. Once you know your pattern, everything else in the job search begins to make sense. You can develop a clear employer-centered objective,

> *Since employers want to hire your future rather than your past, you need to clearly communicate to them your pattern of accomplishments.*

develop keywords that accurately reflect your skills and accomplishments, and write and talk with confidence, enthusiasm, and certainty about what you expect to accomplish for the employer. Whether communicating online or offline, you will present an image of competence.

There are many ways to get at your pattern of accomplishments. At Bernard Haldane Associates our clients use, with the assistance of a Career Advisor, our innovative Success Factor Analysis for analyzing skills and accomplishments and formulating them into a clear career objective. We also supplement Success Factor Analysis with other professional self-assessment devices, such as the popular *Myers-Briggs Type Indicator*®. Taken together, these self-assessments provide our clients with a clear picture of who they really are in terms of skills, motivations, and accomplishments. This information helps them formulate a very targeted objective which guides their job search to the perfect job that is compatible with their past, present, and future. In this sense, there is a good "fit" between them and the job. There's also a high probability they will enjoy what they do and be very successful in their new job.

What Really Works

Our clients come to us because they have a very specific need – find a job that will be right for them. For more than five decades we have worked with hundreds of thousands of clients in helping them realize their career dreams. Our experience with the day-to-day realities of finding jobs has taught us many lessons about what really works when looking for a job. Indeed, our most successful clients are ones who consistently do the following:

1. **Listen and follow the advice of a career professional** (a Haldane Career Advisor) who knows what he or she is doing and who offers numerous tools to make things happen. Being very independent, take-charge individuals, these job seekers often initially resist such advice, but they eventually listen, surrender, and succeed beyond their dreams.

2. **Follow a clear step-by-step process**, based on self-assessment and goal setting, for connecting to the right job.

3. **Formulate employer-center goals and articulate an appealing pattern of accomplishments** that is well documented, and predictable.

4. **Focus on the needs of the employer** rather than on their own employment needs or personal wants.

5. **Communicate likability, honesty, and trustworthiness** along with competence in their area of expertise.

They also are hard workers in finding the right job. They do lots of research, network with dozens of people, write outstanding resumes and letters, follow up, and remain persistent in finding the perfect job. They welcome using the telephone, fax, and Internet to do research, network, and communicate with employers. Most important of all, they know how to sell themselves because they know their strengths, are goal-oriented, and welcome professional guidance. They accept rejections as part of the learning and marketing processes – quickly learn from them and move on to other situations that will hopefully result in acceptances that lead to the right job.

The Savvy Job Seeker

The savvy job seeker is one who is very focused on goals and outcomes. He or she organizes a job search campaign around these sequential steps, which constitute a clearly defined job search process:

1. Self-assessment
2. Goal-setting
3. Researching jobs and employers
4. Networking for information, advice, and referrals
5. Writing resumes and letters
6. Contacting employers and recruiters
7. Interviewing for jobs
8. Negotiating salary and terms of employment

Most of these steps take place in sequence, with self-assessment and goal-setting being the very first steps that provide guidance for all other steps in this process. For example, once you have a clear idea of what you do well and enjoy doing and formulate your interests, skills, and past accomplishments into a clear employer-centered objective, you will be well prepared to complete all other steps in the job search process. Self-assessment and goal-setting provide important direction to your job search. Rather than randomly look for jobs and employers or create a long and unfocused resume of your work history, self-assessment and goal-setting help you focus your efforts in specific directions and clearly communicate to others what it is you have done, can do, and will do in the future for them.

Offline and Online Effectiveness

Ten years ago, most of these job search steps were conducted through the mail, over the telephone, or in face-to-face settings. Savvy job seekers perfected their research, writing, distribution, and interpersonal skills. However, with the cost-effective movement of recruiter sourcing and HR screening functions to the Internet, several job search steps have become increasingly compatible with this online medium.

As you will quickly discover in the following pages, the Internet is an especially effective medium for conducting research, searching for job listings, and transmitting resumes, letters, and other messages to employers and recruiters. It is much less effective for self-assessment, goal setting, networking, and interviewing, although all of these functions can now be performed online with various degrees of effectiveness. As a result, most employment-related websites disproportionately emphasize research, job listings, and resume distribution – elements that can easily be automated for quickly connecting candidates with employers and recruiters. Using search engines and email, job seekers can tap into a wealth of online information and opportunities for conducting an effective job search. At the same time, savvy job seekers recognize that the most important steps to any job search continue to take place offline and primarily involve the use of the telephone and face-to-face meetings. The following chart emphasizes the relative effectiveness of various job search steps that can be conducted both online and offline:

Key Offline Activities	**Key Online Activities**
■ Self-assessment	■ Research
■ Goal-setting	■ Networking
■ Networking	■ Browsing job listings
■ Writing resumes/letters	■ Distributing resumes/letters
■ Interviewing	■ Contacting employers/recruiters
■ Negotiating salary	■ Following up

While all steps can be conducted either online or offline, you are well advised to incorporate and link the two mediums in your job search. In so doing, you take advantage of strengths inherent in each medium.

Offline activities are primarily conducted on your own, over the telephone, or in face-to-face meetings. Online activities are primarily conducted via email and searchable databases. Notice that some aspects of networking, which traditionally have been done via the telephone, mail, and face-to-face meetings, can also be done online.

Individuals, Coaches, and Support Groups

In a good economy, most people can conduct a job search on their own through a combination of intuition and advice gleaned from books, websites, and other resources. While anyone can find a job, few people are successful in finding a job that is compatible with their interests, skills, and pattern of accomplishments. Lacking clear goals and an understanding of their strengths, they end up in jobs that may not be a good fit. After a while, they need to look for another job which hopefully will be a better fit.

Our experience is that most job seekers can benefit tremendously from the assistance of a career professional and a support group. A career professional often provides the following advantages:

- Shares many years of experience on what works and doesn't work for job seekers.

- Helps organize a job search around self-assessment and goal setting.

- Provides a structure for implementing and following up each stage of a job search.

- Offers assistance at each stage, especially with the psychological ups and downs inherent in what is often a rejection-ridden process, and helps motivate the job seeker.

Many job seekers avoid seeking professional assistance because they view it as an admission that they need help. They operate like amateurs with perceptions of being professionals. Accordingly, they wander off on their own with unrealistic expectations and lots of wishful thinking – this process will be quick and easy once employers take a look at my wonderful resume, which I proudly wrote on my own! However, few job seekers put together a great resume simply because they fail to complete the very first "foundation" steps in their job search – self-assessment and goal setting – and they are not talented at writing succinct one- to two-page summaries of their key accomplishments. They should at least see a career professional who can help them with this step in the process. They also would be wise to work with such an expert throughout the whole job search process, especially when it comes to conducting research, networking, interviewing, and negotiating salary. Doing all of these job search steps on one's own – and remaining highly motivated throughout the process – is something very few people can sustain on their own for very long. Knowing that there is someone there to provide advice and structure – a career coach – is very reassuring. It does wonders for motivation and sustained action!

> *Few job seekers put together a great resume simply because they fail to complete the very first "foundation" steps in their job search – self-assessment and goal setting.*

Support groups can also be important when conducting a job search. Knowing that you are not alone and sharing your experiences with others who are going through the same process also help with motivation. If structured properly, with clear weekly performance goals (make 100 cold calls and develop 25 new networking contacts), such groups can serve as a catalyst in organizing and implementing an effective job search. Support groups can range in shape and size from informal gatherings of four or five job seekers to formalized groups of 30 or more which are often sponsored by nonprofit organizations.

Using a one-on-one career coach in tandem with a support group can be especially effective for conducting an effective job search. Experience shows that individuals can dramatically shorten their job search time as well as maintain a positive and proactive orientation throughout their job search when using such resources.

Online Professionals and a CS2K Future

The Internet can be a double-edged sword when conducting a job search. On the one hand, it is rich with employers, recruiters, job listings, and career advice. On the other hand, it is filled with lots of suspect characters who present themselves as "career experts" dispensing what appears to be sound advice and services. Some are free while others charge for their services; most are piecemeal in the sense of offering one or two specialized services. The most prevalent of such experts, who advertise services online, are professional resume writers and resume distributors (resume blasters) and, to a much lesser extent, testing specialists, interview coaches, and salary negotiation experts. You also can use the Internet as a directory to find certified career counselors and coaches in your community who can assist you with various aspects of your job search. Some charge hourly rates whereas others offer a complete package. A debate continues whether or not you should use the piecemeal hourly rate approach or acquire the complete package of services.

If and when you decide you can benefit from the assistance of a career professional, do consider the Haldane network of Career Advisors which are listed in the Appendix of this book as well as through our website: jobhunting.com. We offer a variety of integrated career management services that stress the efficacy of the complete package approach. Haldane clients work with a Career Advisor who assists them at every stage of their job search, from self-assessment to salary negotiations. In addition, we integrate the Internet into each step of the job search process through the CS2K system. A proprietary system specifically designed for Haldane clients, CS2K is a thorough-going Web-based strategy created for job seekers. Designed around the Haldane career management model and used with the assistance of a Career Advisor, CS2K is rich with key databases, job search tools, contact management resources, and managed linkages to employers and recruiters. It's a powerful integrated tool for job seekers who recognize the advantages of working with a career professional.

Following our long tradition as a leading innovator in the career management field, our CS2K system literally moves today's job search to a new and exciting level. By focusing on the individual job seeker rather than employers and recruiters, we've literally refocused Web-based technology to benefit our clients rather than primarily assist employers with their hiring needs. In so doing, we continue our tradition of providing the very best assistance to job seekers which began with Dr. Bernard Haldane more than 50 years ago.

Coming Up

The following chapters include several sites that are part of our CS2K system. However, since most users of this book do not have access to this proprietary system unless they are a Haldane client, we have excluded several sites that are part of the CS2K system but which are not generally available to the public nor free of charge. We've also included other sites, especially those dealing with self-assessment, that are not part of CS2K because they address several key issues that are best handled one-on-one by a Career Advisor. Nonetheless, these sites will acquaint you with the importance of the issues.

> *The CS2K system is the only one that fully uses the power of the Web for conducting an effective job search.*

The Internet offers a wealth of employment-related information and services. While most are free to job seekers, a few – especially those dealing with executive-level candidates – charge user fees. As with anything that comes free, the value of many such sites to job seekers is questionable. Without the assistance of the CS2K system, you'll have to make your own judgments as well as piece together sites which may assist you in your job search. In addition, some sites listed in this book may close or merge with other websites given the volatile nature of today's Internet economy. For example, during the writing of this book, four top mega employment sites went through important changes: Monster.com acquired HotJobs.com and CareerBuilder.com merged with Headhunter.net. We expect such consolidation to continue and perhaps accelerate during recessionary times when employer demand for online recruitment services wanes. Our CS2K system keeps up-to-date on such changes as well as makes judgments about the relative value of various websites to our clients. It attempts to fully utilize the power of the Web for conducting an effective job search.

We're the first to admit, at least for Haldane clients, there is much more to the Internet than what appears in this and other Internet employment books.

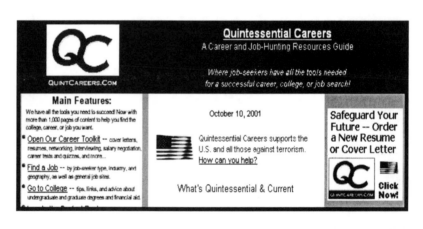

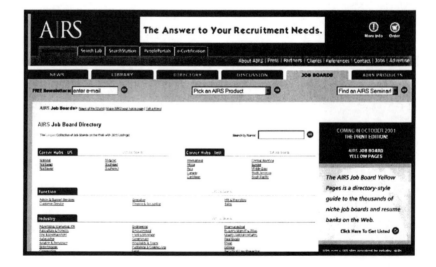

3

Search, Directory, and Gateway Job Sites

F INDING THE BEST EMPLOYMENT-RELATED SITES ON your own can be a daunting task if you are unfamiliar with search engines, search agents, directories, and gateway sites. Knowing which ones to use can save you a great deal of time and effort as well as steer you in the right direction for finding useful websites for enhancing your job search.

Search Engines, Agents, Directories

Search engines, agents, and directories are job seekers' best friends for finding specific information on the Internet or for just exploring information possibilities on the web. Using software with "spiders" that crawl the web for keywords, phrases, addresses, and page titles, **search engines** find websites which fit predetermined search criteria. If, for example, you are looking for graphic design jobs in Phoenix, Arizona, you might choose several search engines (for a wealth of examples, go to bjorgul.com, searchiq.com, allsearchengines.com, and gogettem.com) to look for the following keywords or phrase: "graphic design jobs Phoenix." Each search engine will give you a different mix of relevant websites, which you can then search further.

Operating similarly to search engines, **search agents**, which also are known as searchbots, have the added advantage of also searching various search engines. If, for example, you use the popular search engine Yahoo.com, you might want to switch over to the search agents MetaCrawler.com and MetaGopher.com, which include Yahoo.com in their searches, along with numerous other search engines and websites.

Directories are especially popular with many Internet users and job seekers. Very intuitive and easy to use, directories usually consist of several major subject categories which are sub-divided into hundreds of sub-categories. Numerous relevant websites, which are often compiled by individuals, are listed under each sub-category. If, for example, you are searching for job-related sites, you should look for the appropriate subject or sub-category, which is usually "Business," "Careers," "Employment," or "Jobs." Most directories are found on the front pages of major search engines, such as Yahoo.com, Msn.com, Lycos.com, Excite.com, and About.com. Each of the directory listings will be different, depending on the criteria they use to compile the lists. Therefore, you are well advised to look at the directory listings of several search engines and other websites.

> *Search agents, which also are known as searchbots, have the added advantage of also searching various search engines.*

Altogether, you'll literally find thousands of search engines, search agents, and directories on the Internet. For a summary listing of over 2,600 specialty directories as well as 30 usable search engines that can be activated simultaneously, visit **GoGettem:**

gogettem.com

You may want to frequently reference this site along with the unique **1-Page Multi Search:**

bjorgul.com

These two sites literally function as gateway sites to the many search engines, search agents, and directories on the Internet.

For more information on search engines, including tips on using them, visit these useful sites:

- **searchIQ**   searchiq.com
- **Directory Guide**   directoryguide.com
- **AllSearchEngines**   allsearchengines.com

For information on another category of useful search engines – multi and meta search engines, such as queryserver.com and vivisimo.com, that eliminate redundant listings – be sure to visit searchiq.com.

Best Search Engines

Since there are so many different search engines on the Internet and each tends to yield different results, it is often difficult to determine which ones are the best for your purposes. If you want to know which 99 search engines are the most popular each month, visit Top9.com:

top9.com/top99s/top99_search_engines.html

For example, the following search engines were the most popular in early 2001:

Search Engine	Unique Visitors (x000)
yahoo.com	65,415
msn.com	46,739
lycos.com	22,863
netscape.com	18,816
nbci.com	17,982
excite.com	17,452
about.com	16,291
iwon.com	15,350
altavista.com	14,128
google.com	13,747

Since not all search engines yield the same results, you will need to experiment to determine which are most useful for your purposes.

We especially recommend using these five search engines, with Google.com being the real stand out – the only one your really need:

- Google   google.com
- FAST   alltheweb.com
- iWon   iwon.com
- GoTo   goto.com
- Northern Light   northernlight.com

Key Search Agents

Most search agents incorporate a limited number of search engines in the scope of their searches. MetaGopher, for example, simultaneously searches Yahoo, Google, Spinks, Goto, HotBot, WebCrawler, Go Network, and AltaVista. MetaCrawler includes Yahoo, InfoSeek, Lycos, Excite, and AltaVista. The following search agents are the most popular for conducting such multiple searches:

- Ask Jeeves   ask.com
- Copernic   copernic.com
- DogPile   dogpile.com
- Go2Net   go2net.com
- MetaCrawler   metacrawler.com
- MetaGopher   metagopher.com
- ProFusion   profusion.com

Best Employment Directories

Most major search engines also include a directory section, which has an employment, career, or job subsection. Offering a compiled list of relevant websites and perhaps sponsored links, some of the best sites with employment-relevant directories include the following:

- About.com   about.com
- Ask Jeeves   ask.com
- C4   c4.com

- DogPile — dogpile.com
- Excite — excite.com
- Hotbot.com — hotbot.com
- iWon — iwon.com
- Looksmart — looksmart.com
- Lycos — lycos.com
- Microsoft Network — msn.com
- Netscape — netscape.com
- Open Directory — dmoz.org
- Searchbeat — searchbeat.com
- Webcrawler — webcrawler.com
- Yahoo — yahoo.com

If you choose to regularly visit only one directory, we highly recommend the "Job & Careers" section of the comprehensive search engine About.com, the current star performer. It is well organized by job search and occupational fields.

Popular Employment Websites

In addition to popular search engines, you may want to occasionally check on the most popular employment-related websites as measured by the number of monthly visits by Internet users. The most popular sites tend to have over 30,000 visitors a month, with a few sites attracting more than 1 million visitors each month. A few sites rank employment websites by the number of unique monthly visitors. The following websites offer such rankings:

- Top9 — top9.com/careers_education/ general_employment.html
- Ranks — ranks.com/hom/lifestyle/top_ job_search_sites
- 100Hot — 100hot.com/list.gsp?category= business&keywords=jobs
- Search Engine Watch — searchenginewatch.com

For example, in 2001, the reliable Top9.com ranked the following employment-related websites as the top 9:

General Employment Sites	Unique Monthly Visitors
▪ Monster.com	6,951,000
▪ Jobsonline.com	6,486,000
▪ Hotjobs.com	4,280,000
▪ Careerbuilder.com	1,933,000
▪ Headhunter.net	1,850,000
▪ Jobs.com	842,000
▪ Flipdog.com	837,000
▪ Joboptions.com	829,000
▪ Nationjob.com	342,000

However, in July-August 2001, Monster.com acquired Hotjobs.com and Careerbuilder.com acquired Headhunter.net. Accordingly, these rankings may change considerably in the coming months, especially as more and more employment websites either go out of business or merge with other sites. Structured on an advertising model, which generates revenue through the sale of job postings and user fees to employers, the sites included in these rankings may change significantly from month to month, and especially during a period of economic downturn when recruitment needs decline. While many of the big sites keep on getting bigger and more complex, many of the smaller sites continue to thrive as they provide specialized services to employers, recruiters, and job seekers.

Key Gateway Employment Sites

While using search engines, search agents, and directories will help you sort through the jungle of Internet sites, you also should go directly to several gateway employment sites that can assist you with various aspects of your job search. These sites specialize in compiling some of the best employment-related websites. Several sites, such as the AIRSdirectory.com and CareerXroads.com, primarily focus on the needs of employers and thus focus on recruitment sites, which are primarily job boards for posting resumes and job listings. Other sites, such as Quintcareers.com, Rileyguide.com, and JobHuntersBible.com, primarily focus on the needs of job seekers. The following sites function as some of the most important gateway sites for job seekers and employers:

CS2K (Career System 2000)   **Job Seekers**
jobhunting.com and **bernardhaldane.com**

As noted earlier, this is a very sophisticated proprietary gateway Internet program specifically designed for clients of Bernard Haldane Associates who normally earn more than $40,000 a year, with many earning in excess of $100,000 a year. It's the only completely integrated online program developed for job seekers who need to manage a well organized and targeted job search. Developed for job seekers in the United States, Canada, and the United Kingdom who use the Haldane approach to career management, CS2K is the first system designed specifically to harness the power of the Internet for job seekers. A completely integrated program through its unique WebTie system, CS2K allows job seekers to use a variety of online career tools. For example, they can tap into major databases to conduct online research on companies, employers, and jobs. Through Haldane Online and Sterling Hightower, they make their career profiles available to a select group of employers and recruiters. The system allows users to quickly upload their resume into hundreds of online resume databases. The whole system is designed for conducting online employment research, managing contacts, and marketing one's qualifications – the ultimate networking system for generating information, advice, and referrals. Career Advisors also operate a parallel CS2K system for monitoring client progress and assisting clients at every step in the job search process. The CS2K system eliminates the need to spend hours randomly using search engines, directories, and individual websites in one's job search. It literally cuts through all the online job search clutter in developing a highly efficient and effective job search that saves clients numerous hours in using the Internet as well as hundreds of dollars in access fees for using top quality databases. If you become a Haldane client, the CS2K becomes part of your career management package which you can continue to use over a three-year period. Currently in operation for nearly two years, the system is regularly updated with new and revised linkages and features. As a global organization, Bernard Haldane Associates continues to expand its international scope by including separate sections for clients in Canada and the United Kingdom.

Quintessential Careers   **Job Seekers**
quintcareers.com

Developed by Dr. Randall Hansen, this is one of the most comprehensive sites designed to respond to the needs of job seekers as well as college students. It includes a wealth of career information, advice, and linkages to numerous useful employment websites. Includes job search tools, articles, and tips on everything from self-assessment to salary negotiations. Also offers several online job search services, such as resume and letter writing and distribution, career advisor ("Career Doctor"), bookstore, and a free newsletter. Especially popular with college students and college career counselors, although the site is useful to most every job seeker regardless of education or experience levels.

The Riley Guide   **Job Seekers**
rileyguide.com

Developed and operated by career librarian Margaret F. Dikel (formerly Margaret Riley), this site functions as a virtual library for connecting to hundreds of useful job search and employment resources. Organized around various job search steps – job search preparation, research, resumes and letters, networking, interviewing, and negotiating – as well as incorporating job listings and recruiters, this site is very job seeker-friendly rather than focused on the recruitment and the needs of employers. The site is rich with job search articles, tools, and linkages to employers, recruiters, and employment-related websites that should be useful for job seekers. Indeed, you can spend hours on this site exploring hundreds of subjects listed in the A-Z Index.

Like putting together a huge bibliography of resources into subject categories, the emphasis here is on compiling a large number of linkages rather than on making qualitative distinctions among the various online resources. You'll have to make your judgment as to which resources are really useful. Many of the linkages found on this site also are available through Margaret F. Dikel's popular Internet job search book, *Guide to Internet Job Searching* (NTC/McGraw-Hill).

JobHuntersBible   Job Seekers
jobhuntersbible.com

Operated by author and career expert Richard Nelson Bolles as a supplement to his perennial bestseller, *What Color Is Your Parachute*, this site includes a wealth of information and advice organized around a job search model that is consistent with the work of Dr. Bernard Haldane. Includes a cautionary section on using the Internet in one's job search as well as useful sections on testing and assessment, researching, networking, and writing resumes. The major focus on this site is on the job seeker – helping him or her develop a wise and effective job search based on sound principles of career planning.

AIRS Job Board Directory   Employers/Recruiters
airsdirectory.com/jobboards

AIRS is the largest organization providing training and related services to companies involved with online recruitment. Keep in mind that employers and recruiters primarily use websites for two recruitment-related activities, which they pay for in supporting these sites – post job listings (online classifieds) and search resume databases (resume banks) for qualified candidates. Accordingly, this particular section of the AIRS site includes the largest collection of job boards and resume banks on the Web – 3,258 as of September 2001. By definition, these job boards primarily offer job listings, but many also include resume databases, discussion groups, and related services relevant to job seekers. Employers and recruiters use the AIRS site to identify which job boards might best meet their needs, from general to specialty job boards. As of September 2001, the AIRS Directory included the following categories and related number of job boards which were further sub-divided into dozens of sub-categories:

- Career Hubs, U.S. – 777
- Career Hubs, International – 333
- Function (Executive, HR, Sales, etc.) – 213
- Industry – 852
- Technical – 572
- Healthcare – 162
- Financial Services – 130
- Diversity – 99
- College and Alumni – 85
- Free Agents – 78
- Newsgroups – 168

Job seekers also will find this site useful for identifying where employers most likely post their jobs and search resume databases. Other sections of this site (airsdirectory.com) include useful information on the online recruiting industry in general, such as current recruitment trends and requirements (personality testing, resume rankings, new screening practices) that give job seekers an inside view of current online recruitment issues and practices. While relatively comprehensive, many of the AIRS listings require updating, and some obvious sites are missing in the database. Nonetheless, this is a great site for surveying numerous job board options and especially for identifying specialty or "boutique" sites, which are increasingly playing an important role in online recruitment. Expect to spend hours exploring the many sites listed in this online gateway job board directory.

CareerXroads	Employers/Recruiters
careerxroads.com	

Like AIRS, CareerXroads also is in the business of training HR professionals in using the Internet for recruiting personnel. This site is directly linked to the popular annual directory to employment websites, *CareerXroads*, which is written by trainers Gerry Crispin and Mark Mehler. The site includes a searchable database to more than 600 information technology sites. If you purchased the book, you can access this site to get free updates to the information in the books. While most information on various employment websites is especially relevant to employers and recruiters (number of visitors, costs of posting job listings and accessing resume databases, and focus of sites) who need to decide which sites to use for recruitment purposes, job seekers also will find useful information on which specialty sites are most relevant to their interests, skills, and experience.

Other useful gateway employment sites worth visiting include the following combination of job seeker- and employer-centered websites:

- Career Resource   careerresource.net
- Catapult   www.jobweb.com/catapult
- Careers.org   careers.org
- JobBoard.net   jobboard.net
- JobFactory   jobfactory.com
- Job-Hunt   job-hunt.org
- Job-Search-Engine   job-search-engine.com
- JobSourceNetwork   jobsourcenetwork.com

Remaining Organized and Focused

If you use the many search engines, search agents, directories, and gateway employment sites outlined in this chapter, you should have an excellent overview of the types of employment websites available to assist you with your job search. You'll especially see a major difference between websites that are primarily designed to assist the job seeker versus sites that are primarily designed to meet the recruitment needs of employers and recruiters. Except for CS2K, no websites are designed around the total job search management needs of job seekers. In most cases, you will have to spend a great deal of time clicking on numerous websites and then exploring various sections and subsections to "discover" what information and advice is most useful to you. This is a very laborious and time-consuming activity that often results in losing focus and engaging in random online activities. Nonetheless, this is how most websites are organized and used by job seekers who often find this whole process at best interesting and at worst very frustrating. The more organization and focus you can give this process, the more benefits you should derive from your online job search activities.

4

Self-Assessment Sites

SELF-ASSESSMENT IS USUALLY THE WEAKEST LINK IN any job search, whether conducted primarily offline or online. Indeed, most job seekers start a job search by first writing their resume – without a clear idea of what they do well and enjoy doing. The result is often an unfocused resume filled with historical information comprised of names, dates, job titles, duties, and responsibilities.

Exacerbating a Flawed Approach

The Internet has a tendency to further exacerbate a flawed job search approach by encouraging job seekers to post their resumes online and respond to job postings with a resume. Most employment websites and online resume experts encourage job seekers to write an electronic resume filled with keywords and phrases (in contrast to a conventional resume with action verbs), but the online outcome is usually the same – producing a resume that does not reflect the real interests, skills, and behaviors of the job seeker. The reason is very simple – the job seeker failed to do first things first, which is to conduct a thorough self-assessment *prior to* formulating a career objective, conducting research, networking, and writing resumes and letters.

The First Step to Your Next Job

Self-assessment is the foundation for any well organized and effective job search. Like a ship without a rudder, conducting a job search without a clear understanding of who you are and what you want to do often leads to random and unenlightened job search behavior centered around the use of a poorly constructed resume. You'll eventually get a job, but it most likely will not be the best fit for your particular interests, skills, and behaviors. After all, you never really organized yourself to find such a job since you skipped the critical first step – self-assessment.

> *Self-assessment is the foundation for any well organized and effective job search. You must know yourself before you can communicate to others what you want to do, can do, and will do for them.*

Haldane clients do first things first in organizing an effective job search. The first thing they must do is undergo a self-assessment which gives them a clear picture of who they are in terms of interests, skills, and behaviors. They discover their *pattern of accomplishments*, the single most important piece of information employers want to know about a candidate. Armed with this self-knowledge, our clients are well equipped to specify a clear career objective and then go on to target their research and communicate their pattern of accomplishments to employers, recruiters, and others through networking, resumes, letters, and interviews. Without a clear understanding of who they are, based on self-assessment, they will have a difficult time getting to where they need to go.

Our clients quickly discover the importance of conducting a thorough self-assessment to identify their major strengths, formulate a clear career objective, and develop an appropriate language for communicating their qualifications to employers, recruiters, and others *before* writing resumes and letters, networking, and interviewing for jobs. Whether they conduct their job search online or offline is really not important. It's the direction and content of their communication that really counts. Many clients come to us after weeks of having conducted an ineffective and frustrating job search that began with a resume and ended with lots of ego-wrenching rejections. The pattern of job search failure always seems to be the same – begin with a resume and a complete absence of any self-assessment that could give substance to as well as guide the job search into fruitful directions.

Our clients use a variety of self-assessment devices including the popular *Myers-Briggs Type Indicator®*, which helps individuals identify their preferred work activity and work environment. Our trademark technique is **Success Factor Analysis**, which was developed and refined by Dr. Bernard Haldane during the past 50 years. Best conducted with the assistance of a career professional, this powerful pencil-and-paper exercise yields critical data for specifying one's strengths and developing a career objective. Focusing on analyzing their achievements, individuals discover what they do well and enjoy doing. This exercise forces them to look carefully at their past patterns of successful behavior which they most likely will repeat in the future. They learn to capture this behavior in a language that especially appeals to employers on resumes, in letters, and during interviews. We outline the 10 steps involved in completing Success Factor Analysis, including lots of examples of achievements and Success Factors, in our companion volume, *Haldane's Best Resumes For Professionals* (pages 70-81). In lieu of working directly with a Haldane Career Advisor, this abbreviated examination of Success Factor Analysis should be sufficient to get you started on conducting your own self-assessment.

Weak Testing and Assessment Links

While we cannot over-emphasize the importance of working one-on-one with a career professional at key stages in your job search, you can conduct a self-assessment on your own. Examples of numerous self-directed paper-and-pencil career tests and exercises can be found in such books as *Career Tests*, *Discover What You're Best At*, *Discover the Best Jobs For You*, and *The Quick Job Hunting Map*. At the same time, many employment websites include interactive tests which provide feedback on interest, skills, and abilities. All of these devices provide some useful information to job seekers who need to have a better understanding of what they do well and enjoy doing. The problem comes when moving from understanding to action. What, for example, should you do once you discover that you are an especially creative public speaker who enjoys working in public relations? At this point, you might need some professional career assistance in relating this self-assessment information to other steps in your job search. How can you best incorporate this information into resumes and letters as well as relate it to your research and networking activities?

While some employment websites include self-assessment devices in a "Career Center," "Resource Center," "Career Planning," or "Job Tools" section, assessment remains the weakest element on most such sites. Indeed, there's a curious absence of this element on most employment websites. This raises serious questions about the usefulness of such sites for job seekers since these sites appear to be preoccupied with resumes – getting more resumes entered into their databases and sent to employers in response to job postings. This preoccupation with managing resumes probably explains why there's a near total neglect of the very first critical step in the job search process – assessment.

> *There's a curious absence of assessment elements on most employment websites, which raises serious questions about the usefulness of such sites for job seekers. Most such sites remain preoccupied with managing resumes.*

When an employment website does address the assessment issues, it often does so with self-assessment devices that are self-scoring career quizzes which take two to five minutes to complete. Interesting and fun exercises for many job seekers to take, they are not really serious assessment devices that will give you much guidance for directing your job search nor improving the quality of your resumes, letters, and interviews. Indeed, they may give the test-taker a momentary "Aha" effect – agreement that the test results probably reflect the interests, skills, and behaviors the test-taker already knows about. Many of the mega employment sites (see

Chapter 7), such as <u>Monster.com</u>, <u>Careerbuilder.com</u>, <u>Flipdog.com</u>, <u>Nationjob.com</u>, and <u>Myjobsearch.com</u>) include a testing and assessment section, which may offer specific tests or links to commercial sites (usually MAPP – <u>assessment.com</u>) that provide a combination of free and fee-based online testing and assessment services. Unfortunately, none of these sites treat assessment and testing as an important job search component. Indeed, if one were to grade these sites on their approach to the job search, they would uniformly get a "D" or "F" for failing to include the most important element for organizing an effective job search – self-assessment. But that would be an unfair judgment since these websites are primarily employer-oriented recruitment sites rather than jobseeker-oriented job search sites.

Online Testing and Assessment Services

The following websites offer a variety of online testing and assessment services. Since we are true believers in one-on-one assessment and we have our own preferred devices that have worked well for our clients, we do not endorse any of the following featured sites. We've included them for information purposes only. If nothing else, visit these sites just to get an idea of the importance of self-assessment in your job search and to survey various testing and assessment options. As noted earlier, we use Success Factor Analysis, *Myers-Briggs Type Indicator®*, and a few other well respected professional assessment devices with our clients.

Myers-Briggs Type Indicator®   **Assessment**
Strong Interest Inventory®
(Consulting Psychologists Press)
<u>cpp-db.com</u>

Consulting Psychologists Press publishes the popular *Myers-Briggs Type Indicator®* and *Strong Interest Inventory®* as well as several other testing and assessment devices widely used by career professionals. Strongly recommended for all job seekers, the *Myers-Briggs Type Indicator®* is one of the basic assessment devices used by Bernard Haldane Associates. It describes 16 different personality types and provides reports on individual personality types as indicated by a four letter preference code. The instrument helps individuals better understand, based upon psychologist Carl Jung's personality type theories, why they are interested in various things, including different kinds of work. If you are unfamiliar with this device, this website will give you a quick introduction with its sample reports. The site also includes sample reports relating to the *Strong Interest Inventory®* as well as information on licensing qualifications, certifications, and downloadable CPP software.

Self-Directed Search®   **Assessment**
self-directed-search.com

Each year millions of students and job seekers use John Holland's *Self-Directed Search (SDS)®* to determine their educational and career planning preferences. Next to the *Myers-Briggs Type Indicator®*, the SDS® is one of the widely used assessment devices by career counselors. It classifies users into six distinct interest categories: Realistic, Investigative, Artistic, Social, Enterprising, and Conventional. It is especially useful for someone first starting to explore careers, especially high school and college students. It also has influenced the development of similar assessment devices, such as Richard Nelson Bolles's "Quick Job Hunting Map" which is the central assessment exercise found in **What Color Is Your Parachute?** Operated by the publisher of the SDS®, Psychological Assessment Resources (PAR), this site provides a good introduction into the SDS® and offers a sample SDS® Interpretive Report for someone with an ESC Holland code. You also can take an online version of the SDS®, which takes 15 minutes to complete and costs $8.95 (credit cards accepted). You'll receive an 8-16 page personalized report which includes a list of occupations and fields of study that most closely relate to your interests. The site also includes a useful "Find a Career Counselor" section – just in case you need to consult a career professional – which is linked to the National Career Development Association and the National Board of Certified Counselors.

CareerLab.com   **Assessment**
careerlab.com

Operated by career expert and author William S. Frank (*200 Letters For Job Hunters*) and his associates, this is a serious commercial career assessment site. It offers nine top-quality career assessment devices, which can be taken over the Internet or with the assistance of a career professional:

- *Campbell Interest and Skills Survey (CISS)*
- *Strong Interest Inventory®*
- *Myers-Briggs Type Indicator (MBTI)®*
- *Myers-Briggs Type Indicator – Step II®*
- *16-Personality Factors Profile*
- *FIRO-B*
- *California Psychological Inventory (CPI)*
- *The Birkman Method* (especially for executives)
- *Campbell Leadership Index*

If you want to get a good overview of the best assessment tools used by serious career professionals, be sure to visit this site. One of the real strengths of this site is its up-front admission that you don't just purchase these devices and then go off on your own to interpret the results. Instead, a certified career consultant analyzes and interprets the results and explains the findings in a one-on-one feedback session. The cost of this consultant is included in the price of the instrument.

Personality Online   **Assessment**
spods.net/personality

Designed as a one-stop resource for self-discovery and personal development, this site offers several personality tests. The site includes three categories of tests: Serious Tests, Entertaining/ Fun Tests, and Questionnaires. The three Serious Tests are well worth exploring. They include:

- **Keirsey Temperament Sorter:** Based on the Myers-Briggs Type Indicator®, the Keirsey approach classifies individuals into four temperaments: Guardian, Artisan, Idealist, and Rational. This is a 70-question test.

- **The Enneagram:** Measures personality along nine different scales, each of which are linked to several personality traits. Includes 180 questions which result in being classified into nine different types: Perfectionist, Giver, Performer, Tragic Romantic, Observer, Devil's Advocate, Epicure, Boss, and Mediator. Visit ennea.com for more information on the increasingly popular Enneagram.

- **Personality Profile:** Measures users on 14 different profiles or "types" such as idiosyncrasy and conscientiousness, which are related to several personality traits. Includes an 80-statement test.

Under Entertaining/Fun Tests, The Geek Test, The Nerd Test, and the Maykroner Test have implications for career decision-making.

MAPP™   **Assessment**
assessment.com

MAPP™ stands for Motivational Appraisal of Personal Potential, which is also part of the International Assessment Network (IAN) in Minneapolis (a subsidiary of ZH Computer). This firm has become ubiquitous on the Internet with its numerous affiliate relations with employment sites. Major sites, such as Nationjob.com, use MAPP™ as their assessment linkage. The site offers a free online assessment as an introduction to its fee-based online assessment services. The MAPP™ is an online assessment tool which is designed to measure an individual's motivation toward specific work areas. The MAPP™ works with employers, employees, and candidates. In reference to employers, it profiles positions to determine what type of candidate would best fit the position. Working with candidates, the company produces a user-friendly MAPP™, a "Career Motivational Appraisal," that helps individuals find a career that fits their motivations and needs. MAPP™ also offers several other online assessment and profile services. It produces online reports that can be printed.

PersonalityType   Assessment
personalitytype.com

Operated by psychologists and bestselling authors Paul D. Tieger and Barbara Barron-Tieger (*Do What You Are*), this site includes an online quiz to identify one's personality type. Based on the *Myers-Briggs Type Indicator®*, the assessment approach used here is extremely broad in its application – used to deal with everything from careers to romance.

Numerous other websites include a variety of online testing and assessment devices relevant to job seekers. Many of these sites also include other tests which focus on several types of personal and professional relationships:

▪ **Analyze My Career**	analyzemycareer.com
▪ **Birkman Method**	review.com/career/article.cfm ?id=career/car_quiz_intro
▪ **Career911**	12.32.113.198
▪ **Career Key**	ncsu.edu/careerkey
▪ **CareerLeader™**	www.careerdiscover.com careerleader
▪ **Career Services Group**	careerperfect.com
▪ **Careers By Design®**	careers-by-design.com
▪ **College Board**	myroad.com
▪ **Emode**	www.emode.com/emode/ careertest.jsp
▪ **Enneagram**	ennea.com
▪ **Fortune.com**	fortune.com/careers
▪ **Futurestep**	futurestep.com

- Humanmetrics   humanmetrics.com
- Interest Finder Quiz   myfuture.com/career/interest. html
- Jackson Vocational
  Interest Inventory   jvis.com
- Keirsey Character Sorter   keirsey.com
- OnlineProfiles   onlineprofiles.com
- People Management
  International   www.jobfit-pmi.com
- Personality and IQ Tests   www.davideck.com
- Profiler   profiler.com
- QueenDom   queendom.com
- Tests on the Web   2h.com

Locating a Career Professional

Career professionals come in many different forms and with different levels of expertise. Haldane's career professionals, who we call Career Advisors, normally work with individuals earning in excess of $40,000 a year. Many of our clients are executive-level candidates making more than $100,000 a year. You can contact our offices for an initial free consultation by referring to contacts in the Appendix or on our website – jobhunting.com. As we noted earlier, our services involve a complete career management program, from self-assessment to assisting with resume writing, networking, and using the CS2K online search program. We do not promote a piecemeal approach to organizing and implementing an effective job search.

Most career professionals tend to specialize in particular aspects of the job search – assessment, resume writing, or interview coaching. For example, your local community or junior college will most likely offer fee-based testing and assessment services involving the following instruments: *Myers-Briggs Type Indicator®*, *Strong Interest Inventory®*, and the *Self-Directed Search®*. Local employment offices also offer career services (visit America's Service Locator, www.servicelocator.org, or America's Job Bank, www.ajb.dni.us).

Several professional organizations maintain rosters of qualified career professionals who come in three different forms: career counselors, professional resume writers, and certified career coaches. Some are qualified to administer tests and provide one-on-one counseling services while others primarily write resumes via telephone, fax, the Internet, or mail. The latter group offers excellent writing skills but may know little about testing and assessment nor encourage clients to complete a self-assessment prior to providing information for writing a resume. Whatever you do, make sure the career professional you work with understands the job search process as well as you do.

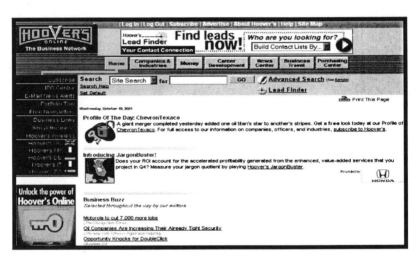

5

Research, Information, and Advice Sites

FOR JOB SEEKERS, THE INTERNET IS AN ESPECIALLY valuable resource for conducting research and acquiring useful information and advice. Indeed, you may find this to be the most important use of the Internet in your job search – acquiring information about jobs, employers, companies, compensation, communities, and relocation. Most information you might normally get through library sources is likely to be available on the Internet and in a much more user-friendly form.

Key CS2K Databases

Haldane's CS2K system is specially designed to provide clients with access to the major research databases for conducting employment research. While some of the databases are free to the public, others are proprietary databases requiring special user-fees and access codes. The U.S. section consists of nearly 60 research databases. Some of the major U.S. databases included in CS2K's WebTie™ channel are:

- America's CareerInfoNet   www.acinet.org
- Bureau of Labor Statistics   www.bls.gov
- Chambers of Commerce   www.worldchambers.net
- Dun and Bradstreet's
  Million Dollar Database   dnbmdd.com/mddi
- Hoovers Online   hoovers.com
- Newspapers USA   www.newspapers.com
- Salary.com   salary.com
- State and Local
  Government On the Net   piperinfo.com/state/index.cfm

Other research databases are organized for our clients in Canada and the United Kingdom. The Canadian section, for example, includes more than 130 research databases. The United Kingdom section includes more than 40 research databases.

Business Directories, Lists, and News

If you're primarily targeting your job search on the private sector, you will find numerous online databases for conducting research on jobs, employers, and companies. The following websites are well worth exploring for research purposes:

CEO Express	Research
ceoexpress.com	

Easy to use, this is one of the richest resources for acquiring information on a wide range of subjects: daily news and information, business research, office tools, travel, and leisure (breaktime). You should be particularly interested in the research section which includes nearly 200 websites classified into 18 categories:

- Financial Markets
- Quotes and Market News
- Online Investor Services
- Government Agencies
- Statistics

- Company Research
- SEC
- International Business
- Banking and Finance
- Small Business

- Investing & IPO Research
- Internet Research & Surveys
- Business Links
- Online Marketing

- Law
- Legislature
- Bankruptcy
- Cutting Edge

You may want to bookmark this website and return to it numerous times for doing research as well as for exploring its many other useful sections.

Hoover's Online   Research
hoovers.com

Hoover's Online maintains one of the best online databases for researching large companies in North America, the United Kingdom, France, Germany, Italy, and Spain. It includes both free and fee-based sections. Its Capsule Profiles provide detailed information on the history, officers, location, products/operations, and competitors of over 4,000 of the largest, most influential, and fastest-growing public, private, and government-operated enterprises. While you can access brief profiles on 300 top companies, access to most of Hoover's database is by a monthly subscription fee. A very useful site if you are primarily interested in researching the largest companies with annual revenues in excess of $1 billion. The site includes several useful data organization and communication features as well as links to employment sections of company websites. Its "Career Development" section includes a Job Bank section which enables users to conduct a meta search for job listings on 300+ career sites.

Dun and Bradstreet's   Research
Million Dollar Database
dnbmdd.com/mddi

This is one of the most popular databases for researching nearly 1.6 million public and private companies in the U.S. and Canada with annual revenues in excess of $1 million. Its linkage to Dun and Bradstreet's International Business Locator provides access to over 28 million global companies in more than 200 countries. Includes a searchable database. Company information includes SIC code, size criteria (employees and annual sales), type of ownership, principal executives, and biographies. Covers everything from small to medium and large companies that voluntarily submit financial and contact data to Dun and Bradstreet (not all do). An excellent source for identifying and targeting companies, including names and phone numbers of key personnel. Individuals and companies must pay subscription fees to access this database and print out company reports.

CorporateInformation   **Research**
corporateinformation.com

This research site includes over 350,000 company profiles in its database. Can search by company name, stock ticker, country, research reports, and state location. If a company is in the database, the site will include linkages to numerous databases, such as Hoover's Online, and reports relating to the company. The state location section includes information on the top public and private companies in each state. Includes many news items and press releases.

@brint.com, The BizTech Network   **Research**
brint.com

This no-frills site is nearly overwhelming with its news linkages and content. It identifies itself as the premier business and technology portal and global community network for e-business, information, technology, and knowledge management. The site includes a great deal of information on relevant industries and companies. Can search for information, which is usually in the form of news articles, about various companies. Includes several useful career resources for information and technology specialists. Rich with linkages to thousands of business and career sites.

AllBusiness   **Research**
www.allbusiness.com

Focusing on small businesses, the directory section of this site includes more than 700,000 business listings which are organized into over 9,000 categories. Companies voluntarily list themselves in this huge directory for the purposes of generating sales leads and locating vendors for products and services. The site also includes numerous useful resources to help small businesses survive and prosper.

BizWeb   **Research**
bizweb.com

This site functions as an online business guide to 46,323 companies which are listed in 207 categories. Just click onto an appropriate business category and you'll find linkages to hundreds of related businesses. For example, under "Service," the "Employment" subcategory yields 551 employment-related firms which includes everything from employment websites and HR consultants to resume writing companies and executive search firms.

Business.com   **Research**
business.com

This site functions as a huge compiled directory to more than 400,000 business websites, which are classified into over 25,000 categories and subcategories. Includes detailed information (news, financials, and bios of executives) on 64,000 companies through its "Company Finder" search engine. Also includes profiles, recent news, and associations of 58 industries. Attempting to become the one-stop shop for general and targeted information on businesses.

EDGAR   Research
www.sec.gov/edgar.shtml

If you want to check the financials of companies required to register with the Securities and Exchange Commission (SEC), be sure to visit the EDGAR database. The SEC requires all public companies (except foreign companies and those with less than $10 million in assets and fewer than 500 shareholders) to file registration statements, periodic reports, and other forms electronically through EDGAR. This site is open to anyone and the information can be downloaded for free. Can search by name, keywords, phrases, dates, and Standard Industrial Classification (SIC) Codes. While not all SEC filed documents are included in the EDGAR database, there are plenty of essential documents to give one an inside view of corporate finance.

Other useful online databases and research tools for investigating companies, employers, and jobs include:

- **Annual Reports**   annualreportservice.com
- **Chambers of Commerce**   www.chambers.com
- **Daily Stocks**   dailystocks.com
- **The Corporate Library**   thecorporatelibrary.com
- **Forbes 500**   forbes.com/lists
- **Fortune 500**   fortune.com
- **Harris InfoSource**   www.harrisinfo.com
- **Inc. 500**   inc.com/500
- **Moodys**   www.moodys.com
- **NASDAQ**   nasdaq.com
- **One Source Corp Tech**   onesource.com/products/
  Profiles   corptech.htm
- **Standard & Poors**   standardandpoors.com
- **Thomas Regional**   thomasregional.com
- **Thomas Register**   thomasregister.com
- **Wall Street Research Net**   wsrn.com
- **Yahoo Corporate Directory**   yahoo.com/text/business_and
  _economy/companies
- **ZDNet Company Finder**   zdnet.companyfinder

Several companies periodically publish lists which compare, rank, and rate the "largest," "top," or "best" companies, people, or places. _Forbes, Fortune,_ and _Money_ magazines include these lists on their websites:

forbes.com/lists
- 100 Top Celebrities
- 200 Best Small Companies
- 400 Best Big Companies
- 400 Richest Americans
- 500 Largest Private Companies
- 800 Best Paid CEOs
- The Billionaires
- Forbes 500s
- Forbes International 500
- Forbes/Milken Best Places for Business and Career
- World's Richest People

fortune.com
- 50 Most Powerful Women in Business
- 100 Best Companies to Work For
- 100 Fastest-Growing Companies
- America's Forty Richest Under 40
- America's Most Admired Companies
- Best Companies For Minorities
- The Fortune e-50
- The Fortune 500
- The Global 500
- The Power 25: Top Lobbying Groups
- World's Most Admired Companies

money.com
- Best Places to Live
- Best Places to Retire

You may also want to regularly monitor several major business magazines which include a great deal of content on companies, executives, and employment trends as well as offer job search information and services. The following websites of business magazines and newspapers are well worth visiting:

Online Magazines

- Business Week   businessweek.com
- Economist   economist.com
- Fast Company   fastcompany.com
- Forbes   forbes.com
- Fortune   fortune.com
- Smart Money   smartmoney.com
- Red Herring   herring.com

Online Newspapers

- Investor's Business Daily   investors.com
- Los Angeles Times   latimes.com
- New York Times   nytimes.com
- USA Today   usatoday.com
- Wall Street Journal   wsj.com
- Washington Post   washingtonpost.com

Online Financial News

- Bloomberg   bloomberg.com
- CNNfn   cnnfn.cnn.com
- Motley Fool   fool.com
- TheStreet.com   thestreet.com

Most of these online publications can be quickly accessed through the front page of CEOExpress.com.

Trade and Professional Associations

If your career interests lie outside business and government, you should seriously consider exploring career opportunities with trade and professional associations. Primarily headquartered in Washington, DC, New York City, and Chicago, more than 25,000 associations function within the United States. At least 5,000 associations have a substantial budget and staff to offer job opportunities for enterprising job seekers. While data on these associations can be accessed through two annual paper directories readily available in major libraries – *The Encyclopedia of Associations* and the *National Trade and Professional Associations* – similar information can also be accessed online by visiting these gateway websites to the world of associations:

Associations on the Net   **Associations**
ipl.org/ref/AON

This site profiles over 2,000 Internet sites that represent professional and trade associations, cultural and art organizations, political parties and advocacy groups, labor unions, academic societies, and research institutions. It provides an abstract of each site and includes URLs and email addresses for contacting the organization. Classifies associations by these subject areas:

- Business & Economics
- Computers & Internet
- Education
- Entertainment & Leisure
- Health & Medical Sciences
- Arts & Humanities
- Law, Government & Political Science
- Regional & Country Information
- Science & Technology
- Social Sciences

Also includes an alphabetical listing of associations as well as a search engine. Operated by the Internet Public Library.

Association Central   **Associations**
associationcentral.com

This site is very active in promoting associations. In addition to providing a searchable database of major professional and trade associations and nonprofit groups, the site includes association news, publishes an online newsletter, and maintains a strategic partnership with the American Society of Association Executives for promoting association activities. Includes upcoming association events, publications, a list of association vendors (Marketplace), and a keyword search. Classifies associations into these 12 categories:

- Arts & Humanities
- Business & Economy
- Computing & Internet
- Education
- Entertainment
- Government
- Health
- News & Media
- Recreation & Sports
- Science
- Social Science
- Society & Culture

American Society of Association Executives   **Associations**
www.asaenet.org

This is the premier organization of association personnel and a gateway site to over 6,500 associations. If you're looking for an association job and wish to participate in professional development activities, be sure to join this organization. It operates its own career center which includes job postings, a resume database, and career services to assist job seekers. Employers and executive search firms regularly turn to ASAE to recruit key personnel for their organizations and clients. This site also includes educational programs, a calendar of upcoming meetings, a magazine and newsletters, bookstore, networking listservers, and several other services for both members and nonmembers. If you are interested in working for an association in the Washington, DC Metro area, you may want to check out ASAE's sister organization – the Greater Washington Society of Association Executives (gwsae.org).

Manufacturing Associations   **Associations**
manufacturing.net

This site functions as a gateway to manufacturing associations as well as manufacturers, from auto, metals, electronics, and chemicals to communication, utilities, technology, and supply chain management. It includes a directory to hundreds of manufacturing associations, a listing of upcoming trade shows, magazines, yellow pages (covers over 60,000 listings for products, suppliers, and service companies), news, top 50 manufacturers, and an employment section (job postings and resume database) powered by Monster.com.

Nonprofit Organizations

The world of nonprofit organizations consists of over 700,000 organizations that employ more than 10 million people worldwide. It's a large but little known employment sector that includes a wide range of organizations such as foundations, charities, and advocacy groups. Like professional associations, many of these nonprofit organizations are based in Washington, DC, New York City, Chicago, and San Francisco. Many also are international nonprofit organizations which function as nongovernmental organizations (NGOs) or private volunteer organizations (PVOs) doing extensive charitable and development work in Third and Fourth World countries. Two websites serve as gateway sites to the nonprofit sector:

GuideStar	Nonprofits
guidestar.org	

This is the ultimate gateway site to the nonprofit sector. GuideStar offers a searchable database to over 700,000 U.S. nonprofits. Each annotated listing includes a profile of the organization, complete with a summary of its mission, activities, employees, volunteers, income, and contact information (mailing address, telephone, fax, email, and URL). Use this site to literally explore thousands of nonprofit employers.

Action Without Borders	Nonprofits
idealist.org	

Action Without Borders is the key gateway site to international nonprofit organizations, most of which operate in Third and Fourth World countries. Its searchable database includes

23,052 organizations operating in 153 countries. The site includes information on upcoming career fairs, a search engine to find services or programs in various countries, hundreds of useful nonprofit resources, and job postings for full-time, internship, and volunteer positions. Offers a free newsletter.

Several other websites provide useful information for researching the nonprofit sector, including job opportunities:

- Access   www.accessjobs.org
- Charity Village (Canada)   charityvillage.com
- Council on Foundations   cof.org
- Foundation Center   fdncenter.org
- Impact Online   impactonline.org
- Independent Sector   indepsec.org
- Internet Nonprofit Center   nonprofits.org

Community and Relocation Research

If you plan to relocate to another community, the scope of your online research also should include community and relocation research. In Chapter 9, we address these issues in greater depth. For starters, explore the following sites:

- 123Relocation.com   relo-usa.com
- Homestore.com   homefair.com
- Forbes Best Places   forbes.com/lists
- Job Relocation   jobrelocation.com
- Relocation Central   relocationcentral.com
- Sperling's Best Places   www.bestplaces.net
- Virtual Relocation   monstermoving.com

Researching Employment Websites

Two websites function as special gateways to hundreds of employment websites. As such, they may save you hours of time trying to research the various sites linked to these two key sites:

JobFactory   **Research**
jobfactory.com

It doesn't get much better when it comes to pulling together lots of job information and services on the Internet. This site links to the top career sites, 1,067 online newspapers, news groups, 1,056 recruiters, and 23,065 employment sites. It also organizes job sites by industry and searches more than 3 million jobs on the Internet. You also can post your resume to various employment sites through JobFactory. Chances are you will want to spend hours working this rich site. Indeed, it could well become one of your most frequently visited sites!

Job-Search-Engine   **Research**
job-search-engine.com

This site will save you hours of time in searching numerous job boards on the Internet. Designed as an "infomediary website" rather than a job board, it searches the top 300 U.S. and Canadian job boards. Just enter one or more keywords relating to the job you're searching for, indicate a state location, and Job-Search-Engine will locate relevant job postings found on these job boards. The site also includes a resource center which links to several career services and specialized job sites.

Research the Career Experts

One thing is for certain – you won't lack for career advice on the Internet. From chat groups to career experts and articles on employment websites, you'll find a fascinating mixture of good and bad advice from everyone who thinks they are a career expert. One expert will tell you to never put an objective on your resume and always handwrite a thank-you note, while another expert will advise you to always put an objective on a resume and never handwrite a thank-you note – it should be typed. So what is one to make of all this well-meaning but often conflicting advice? Whose advice can you really trust?

You should approach much of the career advice you receive on employment websites with a certain degree of caution. After all, many of the so-called experts are self-appointed volunteers with little professional experience. Successful career professionals normally do not participate in these employment websites, unless it is their own site. You might want to visit the websites of several career experts who are known for dispensing relatively sound career advice. Many of them are major career authors, syndicated career columnists, and career specialists with many years of job search and career management experience. Start with these career experts and their websites:

- **Richard Nelson Bolles** — jobhuntersbible.com
- **Paul & Sarah Edwards** — paulandsarah.com
- **Dale Dauten** — dauten.com
- **Margaret F. Dikel** — rileyguide.com
- **Pam Dixon** — pamdixon.com
- **Anne Fisher (Ask Annie)** — fortune.com/fortune/careers
- **Katharine & Randall Hansen** — quintcareers.com
- **Andrea Kay** — andreakay.com
- **Joyce Lain Kennedy** — sunfeatures.com
- **Ron & Caryl Krannich** — www.winningthejob.com
- **Hal Lancaster** — careerjournal.com/columnists
- **Amy Lindgren** — prototypecareerservice.com
- **Fran Quittal** — careerbabe.com
- **Rob Rosner** — workingwounded.com
- **Barbara Sher** — barbarasher.com
- **Rebecca Smith** — eresumes.com
- **Steve Stromp** — daytonclassifieds.com/classifieds/employment/0000stromp.html
- **Paul D. Tieger and Barbara Barron-Tieger** — personalitytype.com
- **Kate Wendleton** — fiveoclockclub.com
- **Bob Weinstein** — suntimes.com/index/weinstein.html
- **Martin Yate** — careerbrain.com

6

Networking, Support, and Mentoring Sites

NETWORKING SHOULD PLAY AN IMPORTANT ROLE in your job search. Indeed, some of the best quality jobs are often found through the process of networking for information, advice, and referrals. Focusing on the interpersonal dimension of the job search, you build an effective network of friends, acquaintances, and strangers by conducting numerous referral interviews that eventually lead to uncovering jobs that are appropriate for your particular interests, skills, and abilities (see *Haldane's Best Answers to Tough Interview Questions* for details on the networking process). Studies continue to show that networking is the most effective way to uncover job leads and get invited to job interviews.

The Web As the Ultimate Net

While the Internet may appear to be one huge job board for identifying job vacancies and applying for jobs online, it also can be an important arena for conducting traditional networking activities. In many respects, in addition to research, the real power of the Internet for job seekers lies in its networking capabilities – it enables individuals to build, extend, and target networks that lead to job interviews and offers. Through the use of Usenet newsgroups, mailing lists, and message boards, you can join online groups for acquiring information, advice, and referrals. By using special locators and buddy finders, you can quickly locate old classmates, long-lost friends, and acquaintances for renewing, building, extending, and activating your networks. You can participate in professional associations and join community-based groups for honing your networking skills and connecting with others.

If you use the Internet for only one thing in your job search, make sure it's networking. You'll most likely discover a lot more job search benefits derived from the Internet through networking than by responding to job postings and putting your resume into online resume databases.

Networking Skills

Networking is one of those wonderful concepts that everyone seems to acknowledge as being important but which few people actually understand and implement well in their job search. If your understanding of networking is a bit fuzzy and you need to brush up on your networking skills, you may want to visit these websites, which provide lots of useful networking information and advice:

- MyJobSearch   www.myjobsearch.com/
                           networking.html
- WetFeet   wetfeet.com/advice/
                           networking.asp
- Monster.com   content.monster.com/network
- Quintessential Careers   quintcareers.com/networking.
                           html
- Riley Guide   rileyguide.com/netintv.html
- WinningTheJob   www.winningthejob.com
- SchmoozeMonger   www.schmoozemonger.com
- Susan RoAne   susanroane.com/free.html
- Contacts Count   contactscount.com/articles.
                           html

Usenet Newsgroups

Separate from the World Wide Web, the Usenet section of the Internet has its own networks, servers, and routers for operating newsgroups. Consisting of nearly 40,000 newsgroups, the Usenet is the world's largest electronic public discussion forum. Individuals with shared interests come together into loose communities to share experiences, ask questions, post alerts, spread gossip, advise fellow members on technical and professional questions, and recommend useful resources. Operating as relatively free-wheeling forums, individuals post messages to the newsgroup and members read and respond to it with various degrees of enlightenment and privacy – most post to the whole community, although some may choose to send private messages directly to the poster's email. If, for example, you are a travel writer, you'll find a few newsgroups focused on the professional interests of travel writers. The discussions may move in many different directions within a 24-hour period, from tips on how to acquire photos online, negotiate travel perks, and sell freelance pieces to travel magazines, to complaints about specific publishers and recommendations on job opportunities and where to post a resume online.

Many newsgroups are very active and educational whereas others are relatively inactive and useless. Some are very small – only 25 members – whereas others can be very large – over 5,000 members. The quality and usefulness of particular newsgroups depend on the mix of members, personalities, questions, and perceived benefits.

Often overlooked by Internet users and job seekers, newsgroups are electronic networking groups which have the potential to generate useful information, advice, and referrals relating to the job market. Functioning like public bulletin boards, newsgroups operate similarly to discussion and chat groups found on many employment websites. If you belong to a newsgroup related to your professional interests, you may acquire a great deal of useful information on what's going on in your industry as well as discover many useful job search tips. Similar to the dynamics of traditional offline networking activities, the activities of online newsgroups are such that you may meet several individuals who will give you "inside" advice on jobs as well as ask you to send them a copy of your resume so they can pass it on to someone who might be interested in your qualifications. For example, if you need salary information to supplement the resources identified in Chapter 8, you may want to pose a salary question to your newsgroup. The response will probably be very revealing, including information on benefits and perks members are currently receiving. You may discover newsgroups to be one of the most useful networking arenas for enhancing your job search effectiveness.

Several websites provide information on how to find, create, and use newsgroups. Start with these major sites:

- **CareerKey**   careerkey.com/newsgroups.htm
- **Cyberfiber**   www.cyberfiber.com
- **JobBankUSA**   jobbankusa.com/usejobs.html
- **Google**   groups.google.com
- **Topica**   topica.com
- **Usenet Info Center** metalab.unc.edu/usenet-i/
                         home.html
- **Questions**   xs4all.nl/~wijnands/nnq/
                         grouplists.html

Google (groups.google.com) is the largest and most popular search engine for finding newsgroups. For example, if you search for "Employment" newsgroups under the "Miscellaneous" heading, you'll find the following relevant discussion forums through this search engine:

misc.business   misc.job
misc.entrepreneurs   misc.jobs

Cyberfiber (www.cyberfiber.com) identifies several job-related newsgroups under its "Business and Marketplace" section, although most links are inactive. **JobBankUSA** (jobbankusa.com/usejobs.html) is an excellent source for identifying job-related newsgroups by country, city, occupational field, and university, although many of their links also are inactive. **Topica** (topica.com) supports nearly 100,000 newsletters, mailing lists, and discussion groups and includes a search engine for locating a group matching one's interest. **CareerKey** (careerkey.com/newsgroups.htm) identifies newsgroups in the United States, Canada, United Kingdom and a few other countries.

Mailing Lists

Mailing lists operate similar to newsgroups but are more structured and have membership requirements. Usually created by an individual who moderates the list, the purpose of these groups is to exchange information and ideas. Depending on who moderates and the quality of the membership, some mailing lists can be very useful for the purposes of networking and professional development. Others often wander off message (tell jokes, ask silly questions, or are dominated by a few individuals who seem to have a lot of online down time on their hands) and degenerate into useless online babble. As a result, many more serious members may ask to "unsubscribe" since they don't have the time nor patience to clutter up their emails with such nonsense.

If you subscribe to a mailing list, you will automatically receive all postings sent to the group. Serious Internet users who know the professional value of online networking will create their own mailing lists. Indeed, you may want to set up, which also means being the moderator, a special mailing list related to your professional interests. Such a group could become a valuable online community for acquiring valuable information, advice, and referrals – the ultimate goals of any networking campaign. If, for example, you earn over $100,000 a year, you might want to create your own mailing list on "Career Tips for $100,000+ Jobs." You would probably attract several members who would be interested in discussing many of the job search and career development issues affecting you and others in this salary category. Discussions might center on such issues as when to use an executive recruiter, negotiating a compensation package, using online recruiters, paying for executive search services, the efficacy of using resume blasters, golden parachutes, provisions in employment contracts, or using career management firms. Accordingly, you may discover that you have created an important network which remains focused on dispensing useful information and advice on key career issues affecting your future.

If you are interested in joining ongoing mailing lists, which are free, check out these two sites:

- **Publicly Accessed Mailing Lists** palm.net

- Topica   topica.com/dir/cid=561

If you would like to start your own mailing list for free, visit these four sites:

- **Coollist**   coollist.com
- **Google**   groups.google.com
- **Topica**   topica.com
- **Yahoo! Groups**   groups.yahoo.com

Message Boards

Many employment websites include message boards which may be referred to in the following terms:

- communities   - discussion groups
- forums   - chat groups

Many are moderated by career experts or site administrators and may include a professional advisor who responds to the various questions or comments. Most of these message boards require individuals to revisit the site to browse through messages and replies. This is often done purposefully to encourage repeat traffic to the site. Some sites include an automatic email reply, similarly to mailing lists, which routes messages directly to your email address and thus does not require periodically returning to the message board site.

Many of the mega employment sites outlined in Chapter 7 include message boards as part of their peripheral career services to job seekers. The most extensive and active message board is found on the **Monster.com** site:

community.monster.com/board

Vault.com also includes several message boards:

vault.com/community/mb/mb_home.jsp

You may find some very useful information and advice by browsing through these message boards and by occasionally posing questions that generate information, advice, and referrals. You may want to include message boards in your ongoing networking campaign.

Building Networks

One of the very first things you need to do in organizing a networking campaign is to identify who is in your network. If you are like most experienced job seekers, you know hundreds of people who might be helpful in providing you with information, advice, and referrals. But you may not know how to find your old college friends or a former teacher or colleague whom you lost contact with several years ago. No problem. Several websites will help you find those long-lost friends within a few seconds. Start with these websites which function as locators:

- **Anywho**   anywho.com
- **Classmates**   classmates.com
- **InfoSpace**   infospace.com
- **KnowX**   knowx.com
- **Switchboard**   switchboard.com
- **The Ultimate White Pages**   theultimates.com/white
- **Whowhere Lycos**   whowhere.lycos.com
- **WorldPages**   worldpages.com
- **Yahoo**   people.yahoo.com

If you were once in the military and have lost contact with many of your old service buddies, use these specialized military buddy finders for building your network:

- **GI Buddies.com**   gibuddies.com
- **GI Search.com**   gisearch.com
- **Military.com**   military.com
- **Military Connections**   militaryconnections.com
- **Military USA**   militaryusa.com

Professional Associations

Professional associations are one of the best sources for networking, especially those that are organized and active at the community level. If, for example, you are in the training field (workplace learning and performance), you should definitely become an active member of the American Society For Training and Development (www.astd.org). Like many other professional and trade associations, ASTD's 70,000 members are found in more than 100 countries and represent more than 15,000 organizations. ASTD also maintains its own online career center to assist members with the job search. But for many members, the real value of this organization is found in attending the monthly local chapter meetings that enable individuals to exchange information and ideas as well as network for professional development purposes. The professional contacts you make within professional associations become key links for building and expanding your professional network. Individuals within that network should give you valuable information, advice, and referrals. They may become your critical links to landing your next job. Occasionally, they may actually hire you!

As we noted in Chapter 5, the following websites will give you quick access to most professional and trade associations:

- **Associations on the Net**   ipl.org/ref/AON
- **AssociationCentral**   associationcentral.com
- **American Society of Association Executives**   www.asaenet.org

Alumni Groups

If you are a private school or college graduate, don't forget your alumni groups. Studies continue to show that an additional value of a college education may be 5, 10, or 20 years after graduation and it often occurs through sponsored alumni groups. Indeed, the real difference in the value of an education from Harvard University versus Stanford University may not be found in the differences in curriculum. Rather, it is found in the alumni networks which are actively promoted by both of these universities. For example, just for MBA's alone, Harvard University sponsors 110 alumni groups with nearly 30 percent of all graduates contributing nearly $2,000 a year to the alumni fund. Stanford University operates 47 MBA alumni groups with over 30 percent of its graduates contributing about $700 a year to the alumni fund. Both of these institutions encourage strong alumni ties. Not surprisingly, many of their graduates find their first job, as well as make future job moves, through their alumni networks. What these institutions do that others may try to emulate is to first recruit smart students and then tie them together into smart and regularly activated alumni groups for the continuing support of their institution and fellow graduates. The networking side of such institutions is one of the most compelling reasons why someone would want to choose them over other institutions which do not value their graduates enough to organize them into active alumni networking groups.

If you are a college graduate and have not done so, you should check with your college or university alumni office for networking information. Many colleges include rosters of former graduates who have volunteered to serve as networking contacts (mentors) to assist other graduates with their job search. Many of these alumni offices are formalizing the networking process through alumni websites. Take, for example, the United States Military Academy at West Point. It has its own searchable alumni database and a military transition employment site (Association of Graduates of USMA – www.aogusma.org) designed to assist graduates with their post-Academy career moves.

If you've lost contact with your college or university, or want to check on alumni networking services offered to graduates, start by visiting these three sites for information on alumni groups:

- **Alumni.net**   alumni.net
- **Alumniconnections**   bcharrispub.com/isd/alumni
                            connections.html
- **Planet Alumni**   planetalumni.com

Women's Networks

More so than most men, many women tend to understand the importance of networking and organize themselves accordingly for job search and professional development purposes. Numerous associations of professionals are organized just for women, especially in the fields of business, engineering, construction, and information technology. The following websites and professional organizations encourage networking among women:

- **Advancing Women**   advancingwomen.com
- **American Association of University Women**   aauw.org
- **American Business Women's Association**   abwahq.org
- **Business Women's Network Interactive**   www.bwni.com
- **Federally Employed Women**   few.org
- **iVillage**   ivillage.com
- **Systers**   www.systers.org
- **Women.com**   women.com

Local Friends and Networking Events

Two special networking groups are worth exploring if you are a business professional who wishes to make contacts with individuals in your field of interest:

- **Company of Friends**   www.fastcompany.com/cof
- **ExecuNet**   execunet.com

Company of Friends **www.fastcompany.com/cof**	**Local Cells**

The innovative Company of Friends (CoF) is sponsored by the popular business magazine *Fast Company*. Organized by readers of the magazine to connect, communicate, and collaborate with fellow CoF members, it consists of 39,000 business people in 150 urban areas around the world who have formed local discussion groups, mentoring and networking organizations, and creative problem-solving communities. Organized into local units, these community-based groups operate discussion groups. Members of the readers' network can build their own personal profile online and use digital business cards to network.

ExecuNet	Networking Events
execunet.com	

ExecuNet is an executive recruitment and job search site which charges executive-level and $100,000+ candidates membership fees to belong to ExecuNet. One of the services offered to members is sponsored networking meetings in cities throughout the United States. This website includes a schedule of upcoming networking meetings or events sponsored by ExecuNet and other groups. Many of the events are breakfast, lunch, or cocktail meetings designed specifically to improve individual networking skills and job search efforts. Participants are encouraged to prepare a one-minute summary of their background, bring business cards and several copies of their resume, and prepare questions. You do not necessarily need to be a member of ExecuNet to attend these networking events. Check out the online networking calendar, which includes information on times, locations, and costs for attending the events.

Job Search Clubs and Support Groups

Several job search clubs and support groups are organized in major metropolitan areas to assist unemployed professionals. Some are voluntary nonprofit groups while others charge for their services. Most of these groups promote networking as a major job search approach. Check these websites to see if these organizations have a group functioning in your community:

- 5 O'Clock Clubs   fiveoclockclub.com
- 40-Plus Clubs   40plus.org/chapters
- Chicago Jobs   chicagojobs.org/support.html
- Professionals in Transition   jobsearching.org

Online Mentors and Coaches

Several employment websites are especially noted for their use of online "career experts" for dispensing job search advice:

- CareerShop   careershop.com
- Monster.com   monster.com
- Quintessential Careers   quintcareers.com
- Vault.com   vault.com
- WetFeet   wetfeet.com

Other sites attempt to develop online career mentoring relationships. **AskTheEmployer**, for example, has been especially innovative in developing an e-mentoring approach to career management. Job seekers and employees, or mentees, work with online mentors who offer their expertise and provide one-on-one advice and guidance:

- AskTheEmployer   asktheemployer.com

Several other groups also attempt to develop mentoring relationships. The following sites function as gateways to mentoring resources:

- Peer Resources   peer.ca/mentor.html
- Find a Mentor   findamentor.org
- MentorU   mentoru.com

Several groups also sponsor mentoring relations for individuals on the job:

- Career Systems International   careersystemsintl.com
- Deliver the Promise   deliverthepromise.com
- Delta Road   deltaroad.com
- Employer-Employee   employer-employee.com

Whether looking for a job or advancing one's career, networking and mentoring relationships can play critical roles. While the most effective networking and mentoring take place in face-to-face settings, the Internet also can play an important role in these relationships.

7

Resume, Job Posting, and Application Sites

T HE MAJORITY OF INTERNET EMPLOYMENT SITES function as job boards and resume banks. Primarily designed as recruitment sites to benefit employers and recruiters, these sites encourage job seekers to browse their online job postings, enter their resumes into the site's job bank or resume database, and apply for jobs online. Largely financed by employers and recruiters, who pay to post jobs and search resume databases, most sites are free to the job seeker. As might be expected, job seekers flock to these sites in anticipation of connecting with employers via an electronic or email resume. How effective they are in doing so remains an unanswered question. These sites do deliver the goods to employers and recruiters – lots of resumes from which to screen candidates.

At the same time, other websites are designed to assist job seekers in writing their resumes and letters as well as distributing them to recruiters and employers. Operated by resume entrepreneurs, who are basically professional resume writers and direct-email specialists, these sites reinforce the important role the resume plays when conducting an online job search.

Resume Mania on the Internet

It's not surprising that many employment websites promote a traditional, and much flawed, job search model, which encourages job seekers to respond to classified ads (called "online job postings") with resumes. After all, employers and recruiters in search of talent primarily screen candidates by their resumes and letters. The Internet enables employers and recruiters to cost-effectively reach a large pool of potential candidates. By posting a job listing on Monster.com or any other employment site, for example, employers can reach hundreds of qualified candidates they would not normally reach by other means. They also can target their search for candidates by specifying the right combination of keywords and phrases when accessing the site's online resume database.

> *Every time you enter your resume into an online database, your resume becomes a valuable asset to the website, which uses it to generate revenue from employers and recruiters.*

The hunt for resumes, as well as the production, distribution, and mining of resumes, has become a big business on the Internet. Since employment websites make money by charging employers and recruiters fees to use their sites, they need to motivate more and more job seekers to visit their sites, respond to online job listings, and enter their resumes in the sites' databases. Some sites also stretch the limits of privacy by developing partnerships with employers who feed these sites with resumes. In fact, every time you enter your resume into an online resume database, your resume becomes a valuable asset to the website, which uses it to generate revenue from employers and recruiters. The goal of most such employment websites is to increase the number of resumes that flow into their sites either as applications in response to job postings or as resources for refreshing and expanding their searchable resume database.

Some employment websites operate a different revenue model. Rather than charge employers and recruiters to post job listings and access the online resume database, they charge job seekers membership fees to use their sites. And in some cases, a site charges everyone user fees – job seekers, employers, and recruiters. This usually occurs in the case of websites designed for executive-level candidates and/or those seeking positions paying more than $100,000 a year.

Struck By Lightning

While we are critical of the job search model promoted by many resume-based employment websites, we also recognize the importance of getting your resume in as many channels as possible. However, your chances of getting an interview based on responding to online job listings and entering your resume into a resume database is probably very low, unless you have a very unique mix of skills, abilities, and experience – akin to being struck by lightning. In other words, you are well advised to browse these sites for job listings and enter your resume into their databases, but don't have high expectations of being contacted by an employer or recruiter based upon such passive job search activities. You may get lucky. But as noted earlier, you should be spending most of your job search time on other

Don't have high expectations of being contacted by an employer or recruiter based upon such passive job search activities. You need to engage in more proactive job search activities.

more productive and high-payoff activities. Set aside some time to quickly enter your resume online and browse job postings, but don't become preoccupied with such seductive activities. Indeed, our CS2K program is designed to help clients quickly enter their resumes into several online resume databases so they can continue pursuing other productive job search activities which involve proactive Haldane strategies centered around their career goals and strengths.

The Structure of Job Board Sites

For a quick overview of job board sites, be sure to visit the AIRS Job Board Directory (airsdirectory.com/jobboards), with its more than

3,000 relevant websites, which we profiled in Chapter 3. Most of these websites have a very similar structure. The simplest sites are strictly **job boards** – only include job postings from employers and recruiters. Usually free to job seekers, these sites allow individuals to search through the site's database of job postings to identify positions that best match their search criteria. Many of these sites also let job seekers apply for jobs online by emailing their resume in response to positions. Some sites, such as the popular Careerbuilder.com allow job seekers to search for jobs on more than 75 different sites in addition to the Careerbuilder site.

Several job board sites add one other important element to their sites: **a resume database**. They encourage job seekers to enter their resume into the site's database by either using an online template or form or uploading an electronic version into the database. Many of these sites also allow job seekers to manage their resume within this database by permitting them to submit multiple versions (usually limited to five) and periodically updating their resume online. Sites with specialized resume databases are especially attractive to employers and recruiters who pay weekly, monthly, or annual fees to access them for screening candidates.

Many job board sites also include several additional elements to attract job seekers and employers. On the employer side, the site might offer testimonials of satisfied clients along with a variety of useful recruitment tools, from fee-based reference checks to recruitment newsletters, articles, sample forms and interview questions, and hiring/firing tips (see careercity.com/human for examples of such resources). But the largest number of additional services are targeted toward job seekers who are encouraged to visit and revisit the site on a regular basis. After all, the effectiveness of these websites is usually measured in terms of the number of "unique visitors" to the sites. Advertising (job posting) and user (access to resume database) rates are largely determined by the sites' "traffic" levels. For example, a mega employment site that gets 6 million unique visitors each month will charge employers and recruiters a great deal more to use its site than another employment site that only has 20,000 unique visitors each month.

Getting job seekers to initially visit, as well as revisit the site, involves more than just having thousands of online job listings and a resume database. Many sites offer a combination of at least five of the following peripheral job search services to job seekers. Most are free features or services which are designed to keep job seekers coming back to the site:

- Job Search Tips
- Featured Articles
- Career Experts or Advisors
- Career Tool Kit
- Career Assessment Tests
- Community Forums
- Discussion or Chat Groups
- Message Boards
- Job Alert ("Push") Emails
- Company Research Centers
- Networking Forums
- Salary Calculators or Wizards
- Resume Management Center
- Resume and Cover Letter Advice
- Multimedia Resume Software
- Job Interview Practice
- Relocation Information
- Reference Check Checkers
- Employment or Career News
- Free Email For Privacy
- Success Stories
- Career Newsletter
- Career Events
- Online Job Fairs
- Affiliate Sites
- Career Resources
- Featured Employers
- Polls and Surveys
- Contests
- Online Education and Training
- International Employment
- Talent Auction Centers
- Company Ads (buttons and banners)

- Sponsored Links
- Special Channels for Students, Executives, Freelancers, Military, and other groups

Monster.com, the largest and most profitable job board on the Web, would be a good example of a full-service website for job seekers, employers, and recruiters. Indeed, it has perfected the art of attracting new and repeat traffic to its enormous site as well as acquiring and mining resumes from numerous sources in addition to the direct intake of resumes from its own site. Through acquisitions of other employment websites, it has become the dominant job board/resume database on the Web.

Once you understand how these job board sites are structured and who primarily benefits from the structure, you should be well prepared to realistically use these sites. Again, these are recruitment sites – not job search sites – which may or may not include a few peripheral job search features and services designed to encourage job seekers to spend a great deal of time on their site with their resume.

Ten Major Players

Given so many online job boards, where should you look for online job postings as well as post your resume online? You have several choices. On the one hand, several mega employment sites, which receive hundreds of thousands of visitors each month, are frequently used by thousands of employers for posting jobs and searching online resume databases. In addition, these sites offer several peripheral job search services. You may want to visit these sites frequently, depending on how useful they appear for your particular interests, skills, and experience. However, because they are so large, you may feel overwhelmed by so many fellow job seekers, employers, and recruiters using these mega employment sites. Indeed, two of the major complaints of many job seekers using these sites is (1) they receive no "hits" from employers or recruiters after being in the resume database for several months, and (2) they have difficulty finding job postings appropriate for their particular interests, skills, and experience.

At the same time, there is a strong trend toward the development of niche or boutique job boards – those organized around particular occupational groups. If, for example, you are a lawyer or other legal professional, you should include a few key legal employment websites in your job search, such as <u>legalstaff.com</u>, <u>attorneyjobsonline.com</u>, <u>lawjobs.com</u>, <u>eattorney.com</u>, and <u>attorneyjobs.com</u>. In fact, employers are increasingly turning to these specialized sites to meet some of their recruitment needs rather than use the huge job boards outlined in this chapter. Many large employers also are strengthening the employment sections of their company websites and bypassing the large job boards altogether. These sites emphasize an important point for job seekers: While size counts, biggest is not necessarily best. We review several important niche sites in Chapter 11.

The following employment websites are some of the largest, most popular, and complex recruitment sites, which also include useful information and services for job seekers. As the major employment players on the Internet, these sites ostensibly offer numerous opportunities to job seekers.

| **Monster.com** | **Mega Employment Site** |
| <u>**monster.com**</u> | |

This is the number one online employment site as measured by the number of job postings (425,000), resumes in its database (nearly 6 million), and unique monthly visitors (7+ million). Operated by TMP, one of the world's largest advertising companies, <u>Monster.com</u> is a very savvy and profitable operation that continues to consolidate the online employment business with its acquisitions of two of the largest employment websites – <u>flipdog.com</u> and <u>hotjobs.com</u>. In addition to its huge resume database and numerous job postings, this mega site includes several job search features and services for job seekers: message boards, career advice, salary calculator, relocation center, and an assessment test. The site also is organized into several interest and professional communities: college students, senior executives, transitioning military, mid-career, nonprofits, self-employed, free agents, and international. <u>Monster.com</u> also operates separate employment sites in 15 countries, including Canada and the United Kingdom.

America's Job Bank   Mega Employment Site
www.ajb.dni.us

Operated by the U.S. Department of Labor, this is the largest and most comprehensive public job bank. It includes over 1.5 million job postings and a resume database with more than 400,000 resumes. Both job seekers and employers can use this site at no charge. Includes blue collar, white collar, entry-level, and professional positions. The site also includes numerous job search and educational resources through its related websites – America's CareerInfoNet and America's LearningExchange. Especially oriented toward assisting individuals in finding jobs, this site includes numerous useful resources for assisting job seekers with their job search through its linkages to both www.acinet.org and www.servicelocator.org.

Flipdog.com   Mega Employment Site
Flipdog.com

Includes one of the largest databases of resumes and job postings because it literally crawls the Web to compile a comprehensive listing of job postings from other employer websites. Also offers a large resume database. Includes numerous linkages to other career sites, such as hoovers.com and wetfeet.com, as well as many recommended resources for both job seekers and employers (career advice, tests, seminars, training programs, compensation, relocation, networking, interviewing, resumes, negotiations).

Jobsonline   Mega Employment Site
jobsonline.com

This relatively new site (started in July 1999) has become one of the most popular employment websites with over 6.5 million unique visitors each month. Includes an online resume database and job postings as well as numerous career resources that are better organized than most websites: career expert, career fairs, company research, cover letters, eBooks, interviewing, online training, relocation, resumes, weekly tips, and a salary wizard (from Salary.com).

HotJobs.com	Mega Employment Site
hotjobs.com	

Known for its famous Super Bowl ads and acquired in July 2001 by Monster.com, this popular site is supposed to continue as a separate entity. One of the most highly visited employment sites on the Web, HotJobs.com includes a resume database and thousands of job postings. The site offers "Career Channels" or occupational fields through which users can conduct a targeted search for job listings. The site also includes a newsletter, community discussion groups, chats, industry resources, relocation and compensation information, job search tips, and office humor. Includes links to affiliate sites in Canada and Australia. The site is expected to offer more career content in the future.

CareerBuilder.com	Mega Employment Site
careerbuilder.com	

This very well organized, user-friendly, and intelligent site is a favorite of many job seekers and employers. Now part of the Tribune and Knight Ridder publishing empire, this site merged with CareerPath.com in 1999. It acquired Headhunter.net in 2001. CareerBuilder.com also powers the career sections of several websites, such as MSN.com and USATODAY.com. Includes a resume database and thousands of job postings. The site includes several unique features, including the handy Mega Job Search[SM] that searches more than 70 other employment sites. Users can target their job search by locations, job descriptions, keywords, salaries, and selected websites. Includes many useful job search tips and tools, weekly features, polls and surveys, communities (campus and tech), and free and fee-based online testing services.

Headhunter.net   Mega Employment Site
headhunter.net

This popular site includes a huge resume database and over 250,000 job postings searchable by keywords, job type, industry, company, and location. Job seekers can post up to five different resumes. Includes an automatic "Jobs by Email" feature, newsletter, online job fairs, a career resource center (mainly links to commercial affiliates), and a clever "Boss Button" which quickly refreshes your screen when the boss is near! Acquired in September 2001 by Careerbuilder.com.

Jobs.com   Mega Employment Site
jobs.com

Another major job board that focuses on two key elements – job postings and a resume database. Job seekers can post their resumes online as well as search for jobs by category, employment type, and/or location. Includes a few peripheral job search elements, such as a "Communities" section (military, health care, diversity, college, temp/contract, part-time); a resource section (articles, advice, and audio/video by Martin Yate); online career assessments (assessment.com); and several affiliate links for checking references (myreferences.com) and distributing resumes by email (resumeexpress.com).

JobOptions   Mega Employment Site
joboptions.com

This site is one of the pioneers of online recruitment – previously known as AdNet and E.span. Includes a large searchable database of job listings and resumes as well as a "Job Alert" feature for emailing jobs that match your interests. We especially like its extensive "Career Zone" section, which includes an automatic resume posting service (50+ sites), job search tips, career advice, articles, self-assessment tests, career coaching, workplace stories, online education and training, career fairs and trade shows, industry and business research, relocation information, and a fun section that includes WordSearch, bloopers, horoscopes, and best boss.

Career.com   **Mega Employment Site**
www.career.com

This very user-friendly and focused site enables users to search for job postings by companies, hot jobs, keywords, locations, and disciplines. Special features for employers include such proprietary programs as CyberFair™, Jobdigger™, Job Hosting, and Hot Jobs™ for recruiting candidates. Offers numerous resources for job seekers: articles, links to other sites, career counseling services, reference checks, women's resources, college resources, career publications, frequently asked questions, and resume writing tips.

Useful Job Boards

You should also consider visiting several of the following employment websites. Most of these sites include a combination of job postings, resume databases, and job search information and advice. Some sites offer numerous linkages to other websites.

MyJobSearch   **Job Board**
myjobsearch.com

One of the most job seeker-friendly websites, this site is all about job search linkages. While it does not have the ubiquitous resume database, its "Job Boards" section makes this a very useful gateway employment site to hundreds of general, regional, and specialty job boards (57 occupational fields). Reviews each general website by ease of use, search engine, and user service. Its Fortune 500 section includes links to the employment sections of the Fortune 500 websites. Each of its resource sections (Career Planning, Resume, Networking, Interviewing, Negotiating, and Relocation) includes linkages to numerous additional resources. One of the richest employment websites for job search resources. You can easily spend hours on this site exploring its fine resource base.

EmployMax	Job Board
employmax.com	

This is not the typical copycat job board and resume database site with a few peripheral job search services included to keep traffic flowing. This up-and-coming site offers several proprietary job search products such as e-Vita Online™ multimedia portfolio and EXPERTease™ multimedia resume. Includes numerous resource linkages for job seekers: training and education, self-assessment, career coaching, and resume broadcasting. Offers job postings and a resume database. Also responds to the needs of employers with useful resources for conducting interviews, checking references, assessing skills, evaluating credentials, and dealing with retention issues. A well conceived website that understands where both job seeker and employers are coming and going.

Nationjob.com	Job Board
nationjob.com	

This popular site primarily focuses on providing quality job postings and a responsive resume database. Includes a free email service for privacy and several anecdotal success stories from job seekers and customers (employers and recruiters). While the site also includes numerous job search resources (assessment, company and industrial reports, online training and certification, resume writing, salary and relocation information, and a few career articles), most resources consist of links to commercial firms selling their services.

Employment Guide's CareerWeb	Job Board
careerweb.com	

This site tends to emphasize technical jobs and community-based employment websites with its searchable resume and job posting databases. Part of the Landmark Communications and Trader Publishing Company empire, the site includes featured employers, a newsletter, career advice, career resource center, affiliate sites, and a bookstore. Its unique ResumeTrader option (costs $29.95) allows job seekers to simultaneously post their resumes to nearly 100 national job boards, including the popular Headhunter.net, HotJobs.com, and CareerBuilder.com, and several recruiters relevant to one's occupation and industry. Offers links to several other CareerWeb-sponsored websites and to their community-based employment print newspapers, *The Employment Guide* (3+ million weekly circulation in major metropolitan areas).

CareerJournal	Job Board
careerjournal.com	

Sponsored by the *Wall Street Journal*, this is a favorite site for individuals interested in executive, managerial, and professional positions. It also links to websites for college students, executive search (Futurestep operated by Korn/Ferry International), and international careers. Includes a resume database and job postings as well as a great deal of job search information and services: salary information, career news, job hunting advice, and tips for success. Includes special sections with articles on executive recruiters and HR professionals through linkages with the Society for Human Resource Management, American Society for Training and Development, and the International

Personnel Management Association. Drawing on its rich database of career articles from columnists of the *Wall Street Journal* and other sources, this site offers one of the best collections of resources for job seekers and HR professionals. A very well designed and intelligent employment website.

Employment911	Job Board
employment911.com	

This site may save you hours of posting your resume and searching for job listings on other employment websites. Designed as a one-stop job site, it allows job seekers to simultaneously post their resumes to more than 3,500 job sites as well as search more than 350 job sites, which include over 3 million job listings. Registered users receive a free Web-based email account, calendar, and organizer for conducting their job search through Employment911. Its "Career Tools" section includes many articles, stories, videos, and links to commercial job search services (resume blasting, online education, references – includes many of the same companies found on other sites).

EmploymentSpot	Job Board
EmploymentSpot.com	

This well organized site provides job seekers, employers, and recruiters with instant access to numerous Internet employment resources. Enables job seekers to search several online employment sites for job postings through its "Jobs Online" section and search for career events under its "Job Fair" section. Includes a wide range of resources for accessing job postings by location and vocation. Also includes special resources for people with disabilities, entry-level jobs, executive jobs, freelancers, internships, minorities, seniors, and volunteers as well as career and employer profiles, career news, salary surveys, resume and interviewing tips, relocation, and much more. Truly a one-stop shop for a wealth of resources to enhance any job search.

JobFactory	Job Board
jobfactory.com	

This is another one-stop powerhouse for job seekers in search of job listings and resources. Its search engine, JobSpider, simultaneously searches more than 3 million job openings by job title and geographic area. Its searchable "Jobsites" section links to over 23,000 employment sites with job postings. The "Joblines" section includes nearly 4,000 telephone numbers with recorded messages about job openings. JobFactory also reviews the top 250 career sites on the Internet; links to classified job advertisements at 1,067 newspapers in the U.S., Canada, Asia, and Europe; includes 1,056 recruiters with online job postings; and links to employment websites sorted by industry. You can literally spend days working this site for job contacts and resources. One of the richest employment websites available.

Vault.com	Job Board
vault.com	

This is one of the richest websites for job seekers who want to post their resumes online, browse job postings, and use a variety of online job search services for researching employers and improving job search skills. Designed to be a comprehensive recruitment and job search site, Vault.com includes numerous message boards organized by industry, career topic, and university; career experts; books and articles; relocation tools; salary calculator; career stories; networking center; coaching and counseling services; resume review section; and special sections focusing on finance, law, and consulting jobs. Somewhat overwhelming, this ambitious employment website goes far beyond the typical job board site of job postings and resume databases.

WetFeet.com   Job Board
wetfeet.com

While this site does not include a resume database, it offers
numerous job postings and a rich database of job search information and advice. WetFeet is well noted for generating a great
deal of career content, which it syndicates to other employment
websites. It conducts research and publishes pricey reports
("Insider's Guides") which can be purchased online as downloadable ebooks ($14.95) or print versions ($24.95). Includes
a company research section, salary surveys, job search advice
and tips, discussion boards, articles, and a free newsletter. Also
has a special internships section for students (powered by
InternshipPrograms.com). It you combine this site with Vault.
com, you'll acquire a great deal of unique online career content
that is not generally available on other employment websites.

Net-Temps   Job Board
net-temps.com

This is one of the most popular sites for temporary and part-
time job seekers. It includes over 80,000 contract and direct
jobs as well as more than 6,500 recruiters. The jobs represent
several professional fields including accounting and finance,
administrative and clerical, engineering, health care, legal, IT,
management, marketing, and sales. Job seekers can post their
resumes online as well as search for job listings. Includes a
"Talent Center" for contract and full-time candidates and a
weekly newsletter with information, tips, advice, interviews,
and resources to assist job seekers.

4Work   Job Board
4work.com

If you're mainly interested in browsing online job postings and
receiving updates on new job listings that match your particular

interests, skills, and experience and you are concerned about the privacy of resume databases, this site will appeal to you. It specializes in delivering job updates to its subscribers. Nearly 300,000 individuals use the site's confidential "Job Alert!" email service to receive free daily updates of new job listings. In fact, the site purposefully uses the "Job Alert!" approach – a personal job search agent for greater privacy – rather than a searchable resume database. This site also specializes in volunteer jobs and internships (with nearly 100,000 registered users) through its website 4laborsoflove.org.

BestJobsUSA	Job Board
bestjobsusa.com	

While this is another job posting and resume database site, unlike most such sites it's very rich with information, tips, and advice for job seekers. Includes sections on best jobs, best employers, career fairs, trade shows, city information, corporate profiles, college students, career links, and a variety of career resources offered by commercial vendors. This site is part of Recourse Communications, Inc., which publishes the employment newspaper *Employment Review*. Articles from the newspaper are included on this site.

Management Recruiters International	Job Board
brilliantpeople.com	

This site is operated by Management Recruiters International (MRI), which claims to be the world's largest executive search firm with more than 1,000 offices and 5,000 search professionals in North America, Europe, and Asia. Includes a resume database, job postings, MRI recruiters, and application tracking system. Offers job seekers career assistance through an online training center, job search articles, salary wizard, and relocation tools. Free to executive-level candidates, this site feeds into the company's network of executive recruiters and headhunters. When you use this site, keep in mind that you are primarily marketing yourself through Management Recruiters International – not other executive search firms.

Career Shop   **Job Board**
careershop.com

This is another popular recruitment site which offers three main services for employers, recruiters, and job seekers – a resume database, job postings, and a Personal Job Shopper that emails matching job announcements to candidates. Includes several useful resources for job seekers, such as a career doctor (linked to quintcareers.com), training, career links, salary calculator (through salary.com), and relocation wizard (through homefair.com).

Job Sleuth   **Job Board**
jobsleuth.com

This is a one-stop shop, or portal, for browsing a huge number of job postings – over 4.5 million. Using spider software, the site literally searches other websites for such postings. Instead of offering a resume database, the site includes a free email report that automatically sends job seekers new job announcements matched to their interests, skills, and experience. Job seekers can post their resumes to several other sites through Job Sleuth. Includes several useful career tools (resume, salary, relocation, assessment, and references through commercial vendor links), career news, links to other career sites, and a "Career Workshop" section with job horror stories, job trivia, job tips, weekly pool, and a job checklist. Includes links to several other "Sleuth" sites, such as companysleuth.com and entertainment.sleuth.com, and databases of articles through Electric Library (encyclopedia.com).

JobSniper   Job Board
jobsniper.com

This site quickly searches multiple sites in the U.S., Canada, and the United Kingdom which include more than 3 million jobs. Job seekers can search by keywords and location (city and state). Includes numerous job hunting resources: research sites, career fairs, recruiting and HR sites, industry-specific sites, employment websites, job search portals, and IT and business sites. Also includes linkages to European, Asian, Latin American, and African career sites. A very useful one-stop shop for discovering hundreds of useful online employment resources.

Career City   Job Board
careercity.com

This is another one-stop shop for browsing millions of online job postings. Using spider software, the site extracts job postings from hundreds of other employment websites. The site also includes a resume database, company profiles, a diversity job center, job search advice and tips, a career planning section, and a human resources center (one of the best on the Web). Its online bookstore only includes career books published by Adams Media, which is the parent company of careercity.com. The "HR Center" is well worth visiting to review the thinking and approaches of recruiters – includes examples of job offer and rejection letters and sample interview questions for different job fields. Indeed, review the sample questions which you may be asked in the job interview.

JobOpps.net   Job Board
jobopps.net

The main strength of this site is its thousands of job postings that can be searched by company, title, industry, and location. The site also includes numerous job search resources (mainly links to other websites), success stories, list of upcoming career fairs, career news, salary information (from salary.com), and featured jobs ("Top Jobs").

Brass Ring   **Job Board**
brassring.com

This site primary focuses on three key job search and recruitment elements for high-tech jobs: job postings, resume database, and career events (job fairs). Its focus on offline career events, which are held in the U.S., Canada, Germany, and the Netherlands, separates this site from most other employment websites that are strictly online operations. Designed for high-tech professionals, this well organized site serves as an information and career portal. It includes nearly 500,000 resumes in its database and offers more than 70,000 positions in over 1,600 companies. It also includes a huge database of over 600,000 technology and career articles as well as featured cities and companies, a free newsletter, and a CyberLibrary. One of the richest employment websites with both online and offline resources for conducting an effective job search with high-tech firms.

JobBankUSA   **Job Board**
jobbankusa.com

This well organized and attractive site provides a rich assortment of services and features. In addition to its searchable job postings and resume database, it includes a "Job Agent" that emails new job postings to job seekers as well as a fee-based resume broadcast feature (through resumebroadcaster.com) for emailing your resume to over 9,000 employers and recruiters. Its career resource section includes Fortune 500 jobs, occupational guide, industry associations, hot companies, newsgroups, career fairs, assessment tools, relocation tools, career articles, resume samples, news sources, links to partner sites, and a free

Instant Reference Checking service. Other useful services include email lists, free email, yellow and white pages, city and business guide, classifieds, and international linkages.

CareerTV	Job Board
careertv.net	

This rather unusual site merges broadcast television and the Internet by presenting the CareerTV television show in streaming video. Includes representatives of recruiting companies and job listing in video. The site also functions as a portal to career-related websites and online job search tools. Job seekers can search job postings and post their resume online as well as attend virtual job fairs, acquire training, check on career advice, and link to other employment websites through linkages with careershop.com.

Career Magazine	Job Board
careermag.com	

This site is especially noted for its rich collection of job search resources: job search tips, articles, message boards, tools, links, free email, diversity, products, and services. Includes a searchable resume database, job postings, a job match agent, relocation services, and separate sections for employers, recruiters, consultants, and college students.

Employers Online	Job Board
employersonline.com	

Primarily offering job postings and a resume database, this site focuses on jobs and candidates in the following fields: sales/ marketing, engineering/technical, computer/informational technology, professional/executive, and medical/health. Includes links to other employment-related websites.

WantedJobs   **Job Board**
wantedjobs.com

Structured as a one-stop job posting site, WantedJobs allows job seekers to simultaneously search over 250 websites that contain more than 3 million jobs. Offers several job search services as well as linkages to its sites in Canada and the United Kingdom. Also includes relocation, housing, financial, and travel services.

MindFind   **Job Board**
mindfind.com

Primarily focuses on job postings and a resume database. In addition to posting their resumes online, job seekers can search job postings on over 200 websites simultaneously.

JobExchange   **Job Board**
employmentwizard.com

This site primarily focuses on searchable job postings and a resume database. Its free "My Wizard" service lets job seekers develop an online resume and cover letter for online applications. Offers resource links to several other websites.

RecruitUSA   **Job Board**
recruitusa.com

Another resume database and job posting site. Includes an alphabetical listing of company websites which are "sponsors" of RecruitUSA. A "Get Local" section offers linkages to state sponsors and state employment services.

The following employment websites also offer a variety of resume databases and/or job postings which you may want to check out for your own job search purposes:

■ 1-Jobs.com	1-jobs.com
■ 6FigureJobs	sixfigurejobs.com
■ Advance Careers	advancecareers.com
■ America's Preferred Jobs	preferredjobs.com
■ BusinessWeekOnline	businessweek.com/careers/ index.htm
■ CampusCareerCenter	campuscareercenter.com
■ Career Avenue	careeravenue.com
■ CareerBuzz	careerbuzz.com
■ CareerExchange	careerexchange.com
■ Careerfile	careerfile.com
■ CareerMart	careermart.com
■ Career Marketplace	careermarketplace.com
■ CareerSite	careersite.com
■ Classifieds2000	classifieds2000.com
■ CollegeRecruiter	collegerecruiter.com
■ ComputerJobs	computerjobs.com
■ Craig's List	craigslist.com
■ Dice.com	dice.com
■ Employment Wizard	employmentwizard.com
■ ExecuNet	execunet.com
■ Experience.com	experience.com
■ Free Community	freecommunity.com
■ GotAJob	gotajob.com
■ Guru.com	guru.com
■ HireAbility	hireability.com
■ HireStrategy	hirestrategy.com
■ IT Careers	itcareers.com
■ Job Anywhere	jobanywhere.com
■ JobCircle	jobcircle.com
■ JobDirect	jobdirect.com
■ Jobnet	jobnet.com
■ JobStar	jobstar.org
■ JobTrak	jobtrak.com

- Job Web   jobweb.com
- Jumbo Classifieds   jumboclassifieds.com
- kForce.com   kforce.com
- Netshare   netshare.com
- ProHire   prohire.com
- Washington Post   washingtonjobs.com
- Workopolis (Canada)   workopolis.com

Resume Writing

Writing a one- to two-page resume can be one of the most difficult job search tasks, especially if you are not familiar with the basic rules of effective resume writing. If you want to write a resume on your own, you should visit these sites which include articles and tips on resume writing in their "Career Resources" or "Resource Center" sections:

- Monster.com   resume.monster.com
- America's CareerInfoNet   www.acinet.org/acinet
- JobStar   jobstar.org/tools/resume
- CareerBuilder   careerbuilder.com
- Quintessential Careers   quintcareers.com
- Wetfeet   wetfeet.com
- Jobsonline   jobsonline.com
- WinningTheJob   www.winningthejob.com
- MyJobSearch   myjobsearch.com
- Resumesion   resumesion.com

Several websites featured in this chapter include links to commercial firms that offer resume writing and distribution services. Vault.com offers a free online resume critique service. Professional resume writers, such as Rebecca Smith, include useful advice on writing an electronic resume (eresumes.com). Resumesion.com specializes in producing interactive resumes.

Our experience is that most job seekers can benefit from the assistance of a career professional who provides needed focus and assists in developing each section of the resume. Based on Haldane principles – which include assessing strengths, specifying key accomplishments, and developing a career objective – our Career Advisors assist clients in developing a powerful Haldane-principled resume. The principles and corresponding examples are outlined in our companion volume, ***Haldane's Best Resumes For Professionals***.

The resume writing business is a big business, which even includes its own professional associations that self-certify their members. It's also a quick, easy, and suspect business – much like the proverbial 24-hour tailored suit made in Hong Kong: it may look good on its first day out, but it often quickly unravels after a little wear and tear. Indeed, many of these resumes don't wear very well after making an initial positive impression.

If you decide to hire a professional resume writer, you'll find different levels of resume writing services which usually run from $200 to $800 per resume. Most of these resume writers interview clients over the telephone or by email to gather basic data on their educational background, work history, skills, and accomplishments. Within a day or two they produce a one- to two-page resume.

Each professional resume writer has his or her own approach to resume writing. The quality and effectiveness of such resumes will differ from one writer to another. Few of these writers, however, are career professionals who develop resumes based upon a thorough analysis of a client's skills, abilities, accomplishments, and goals. To do so would take a great deal more time (more than a week) and expertise than allotted for such quick and easy production. Many of these professional resume writers use canned formats and language which, after a while, look like many other professionally produced resumes: initially look great but may not go very far with employers.

If you decide to use a professional resume writer, you should shop around to find one that has many satisfied clients – they produce resumes that really work in generating job interviews. You might start with the following associations of career professionals that are top heavy with professional resume writers:

- **Professional Association of Resume Writers and Career Coaches**   www.parw.com

- **Professional Resume Writing and Research Association**   prwra.com

- National Resume
  Writers' Association   nrwa.com

- Career Masters Institute   cminstitute.com

The NetWorker Career Services' (NCS) website includes an online directory of professional resume writers, which reveals their fees, years of experience, and certification as well as indicates whether they offer samples and free resume critiques:

careercatalyst.com/resume.htm

Many of the following websites of professional resume writers offer a free resume critique prior to charging $200 to $800 for their resume writing services:

- A&A Resume   aandaresume.com
- A-Advanced Resume Service   topsecretresumes.com
- Advanced Career Systems   resumesystems.com
- Advanced Resumes   advancedresumes.com
- Advantage Resume   advantageresume.com
- Best Fit Resumes   bestfitresumes.com
- Cambridge Resume Service   cambridgeresume.com
- CareerConnection   careerconnection
- Career Resumes   career-resumes.com
- CertifiedResumeWriters   certifiedresumewriters.com
- eResume   eresumes.com
- e-resume.net   e-resume.net
- Executiveagent.com   executiveagent.com
- Free-Resume-Tips   free-resume-tips.com
- Impact Resumes   impactresumes.com
- Leading Edge Resumes   leadingedgeresumes.com
- Resume Agent   resumeagent.com
- Resume.com   resume.com
- Resume Creators   resumecreators.com
- ResumeMaker   resumemaker.com
- Resume Writer   resumewriter.com
- WSACORP.com   www.wsacorp.com

While we do not endorse these writing businesses, especially since few of these entrepreneurs are career professionals, sampling their websites will give you some idea of your online options for acquiring such services. These are only a few of the many such resume writing services available to job seekers. Again, we caution you about producing a nice-looking resume that may not reflect what you do well and enjoy doing – the key issues in producing an effective Haldane-principled resume. Most professional resume writers can only deal with the superficial aspects of your skills and experience – what you may tell them in a 15 to 30 minute telephone conversation or in an email or fax. They do not produce magic pills that generate interviews and job offers. The quality of their work reflects, in large part, the quality and organization of information you give them about yourself.

Resume Distribution

Online resume distribution has also become a big business. For example, on several websites featured in this chapter, you will notice resume distribution or resume blasting as an add-on fee-based service. This usually consists of a linkage to a commercial firm that specializes in sending resumes to hundreds or thousands of employers and recruiters. Their distribution focus is on recruiters since many recruiters are constantly in search of new resumes to replenish their aging supply of resumes. For example, Resumezapper.com, one of the largest online resume distribution firms, informs job seekers how their service works. They only blast resumes to third-party recruiters and search firms – none go directly to employers. In fact, most of their candidates prefer being marketed to employers through executive recruiters. Recruiters, in turn, sign up with the resume distribution firm to receive free resumes which are filtered by marketing criteria. Not surprisingly, most resume distribution services blast resumes almost solely to recruiters or headhunters. A few such services, such as hotresumes.com, also will blast resumes to websites that operate resume databases. Such services ostensibly will save you time in entering your resume into each database.

Most resume distribution firms charge the job seeker fees for their services. These may range from a low of $59.95 to blast your resume to 1,000 employers or recruiters to over $4,000 to reach thousands of employers and recruiters. The problem with most resume blasting services is that you really don't know who the actual recipients will be and whether or not they have any interest in your qualifications. For example, if you pay $129.95 to have your resume distributed to 10,000 employers and recruiters, what percentage of recipients are really interested in your qualifications? If recipients use filters in receiving resumes, what percentage or number of them will actually "request" your resume? In addition, few employers are interested in receiving what is essentially junk mail – an unsolicited resume from someone who paid a company to engage in a direct-mail exercise. In reality, it is recruiters – executive search firms and headhunters – who sign up with a resume blasting firm to receive free resumes.

If you have unique qualifications that are likely to be of interest to recruiters, you might want to consider using such resume distribution services to reach your targeted audience. Most firms include anecdotal testimonials ("success stories") of job seekers who have been very successful in using their services. The emphasis here should be on "anecdotal" and "stories." Your success will most likely depend on several factors, with "luck" being at the top of the list. Furthermore, we have no evidence to indicate that the $1,000 or $3,000 resume blasting service is any more effective than the $59.95 service. In either case, you are paying for a service that is most likely sending your resume to recruiters who build their database for marketing candidates to employers. There is a good chance you may never get a positive response – an actual interview with an employer – from such services.

Knowing full well that the odds of getting a positive response from such resume blasting services is probably very low, you may still want to take your chances by investing in such a service. Shop around to get some sense of how these services are structured and operate in practice. It's probably best to approach these services with low expectations. But like the lottery, you may get lucky!

Similar to resume writing services, we do not endorse any of the following resume distribution services. We present these URLs solely for informational purposes. If you visit a few of these sites, you'll get a good idea of the various services and cost options. You'll have to probe these sites further to get evidence of effectiveness that goes beyond the anecdotal. Most should be able to tell you what percentage of employers versus recruiters are in their database and whether or not they filter resumes and how these filters might affect the distribution of your resume.

- BlastMyResume — blastmyresume.com
- CareerPal — careerpal.com
- Careerxpress.com — careerxpress.com
- E-cv.com — e-cv.com
- Executiveagent.com — executiveagent.com
- HotResumes — hotresumes.com (posts to multiple job boards)
- Job Search Page — jobsearchpage.com (international focus)
- Job Village — jobvillage.com
  - (Resume Agent) — (resumeagent.com)
  - (Resumeshotgun) — (resumeshotgun.com)
- ResumeBlaster — resumeblaster.com
- Resume Booster — resumebooster.com
- ResumeBroadcaster — resumebroadcaster.com
- Resume Carpet Bomber — resumecarpetbomber.com
- Resume Path — resumepath.com
- ResumeSubmit — www.careerxpress.com
- ResumeZapper — resumezapper.com
- ResumeXpress — resumexpress.com
- RocketResume — rocketresume.com
- See Me Resumes — seemeresumes.com
- Your Missing Link — yourmissinglink.com
- WSACORP.com — www.wsacorp.com

Put Resumes in Perspective

The preoccupation of employment websites with resumes – be it operating a resume database, offering a special job alert email program, responding to job postings with your resume, writing resumes, or blasting resumes to recruiters and employers – tends to promote a much flawed job search approach. While it is in the interests of employers and recruiters to acquire and screen as many resumes (candidates) as possible, it is not necessarily in your interests to focus so much time and effort on managing your resume. Whatever you do, make sure you have done the necessary preliminary work prior to writing and distributing your resume through these online services and channels. You should be in control of your job search by producing a first-class resume that truly reflects what you do well and enjoy doing. Most important of all, you should be proactive in controlling the distribution of your resume rather than play a passive role in waiting to be "discovered" by employers and recruiters who find you in a resume database based upon a keyword search. A Haldane-based job search is one that is focused around your goals and strengths as well as placing you in primary control of the job finding process. You do this by doing first things first – key job search steps which are outlined in Chapters 2, 4, 5, and 6.

8

Interview and Compensation Sites

W HILE THE RESUME MAY BE THE MAIN FOCUS OF most employment websites, it is by no means the most important element to getting a job. What counts the most is the job interview – no interview, no job offer, no salary negotiations, no job. Some employment websites include a few tips or articles in their resource or career center section on how to interview for a job. But for the most part, few sites provide useful information on how to best handle the all-important job interview, from preparation and answering/asking specific questions to following up, accepting an offer, and negotiating compensation. Nonetheless, you will find a few websites that can assist you at this critical stage of your job search.

Interview Preparation

Several of the major employment sites include useful information on interview preparation. This usually takes the form of short one- to two-page articles on interview "do's" and "don'ts," mistakes to avoid, questions employers often ask, and questions candidates should ask. Most sites include these articles or tips in their career advice, job tips, or resource center sections. They also may include a career coach, job expert, or career doctor to field such questions from visitors who are facing a job interview. The following sites are especially noted for including a good collection of job interview tips, articles, and advice:

▪ Monster.com	interview.monster.com
▪ MyJobSearch	myjobsearch.com/interviewing.html
▪ Quintessential Careers	quintcareers.com/intvres.html
▪ Wetfeet.com	www.wetfeet.com/advice/interviewing.asp
▪ CareerCity	careercity.com
▪ The Riley Guide	rileyguide.com/interview.html
▪ CareerJournal	careerjournal.com
▪ Jobweb	www.jobweb.com/Resources/Library/Interviews_Resumes/default.htm
▪ Careerbuilder.com	careerbuilder.com/gh_int.html
▪ Careermag.com	careermag.com
▪ Vault.com	vault.com
▪ WinningTheJob	www.winningthejob.com

A few sites also include virtual and interactive interview sections which may score how well you do in answering a series of questions or critique your performance. Monster.com's "Interview Center," for example, includes several virtual interviews for different occupational fields, from finance to technology. Most of the online interview advice is free, although a few sites, such as WSACorp.com, charge fees for providing online interview coaching assistance.

Preparing for an interview involves more work than reading articles and tips or taking quizzes from books or online. At the very least, it involves face-to-face verbal and nonverbal communication which, in the end, is what a job interview is all about. Not surprising, the Internet is a less than perfect medium for preparing for a job interview. It can be useful, but it should be used to supplement offline preparation efforts.

The following websites provide specialized assistance in dealing with various aspects of the job interview:

Monster.com	**Job Interviews**
interview.monster.com	
content.monster.com/jobinfo/interview	

This site provides two of the most extensive interview preparation sections of any website. Its "Interview Center" includes virtual interviews for 12 different career areas and several articles focusing on different stages and aspects of the job interview process – from nonverbal communication to follow-up activities. Its "Career Center" section includes a few useful articles and tips relating to job interviews.

JobInterview.net	**Job Interviews**
job-interview.net	

If you're looking for lots of sample interview questions along with tips for interview success, this site is loaded with this type of information. It includes numerous practice questions, mock job interviews, 900+ sample questions for 41 job functions, expert interview advice, a seven-step interview plan, and a downloadable ($16.95) interview preparation book. Most of the material on this site is taken from Matt and Nan DeLuca's two interview books: ***Best Answers to the 201 Most Frequently Asked Interview Questions*** and ***More Best Answers to the 201 Most Frequently Asked Interview Questions***. The site also includes interview advice for employers and recruiters. In fact, you might want to prepare for your next job interview by reviewing the employer-oriented interview advice taken from Del J. Still's book, ***High Impact Hiring***. Combine this with the seasoned interview advice given to employers on the CareerCity website (careercity.com), and you should have a good "inside" view of what the interviewer is looking for in the job interview.

JobReviews.com   Job Interviews
jobreviews.com

Here's where the Internet really demonstrates its usefulness in reference to both job interviews and company research. This website is for anyone interested in gaining insights from job seekers who have recently gone through job interviews with companies. Go to the "Recent Interview Reviews" section to find reviews of interviews for more than 500 companies (jobreviews.com/cgi-bin/getsection.pl?select+interview). Here, job seekers share their observations about the interview process and the companies. The interview "stories" cover companies in the following categories:

- Accounting
- Advertising
- Computer Hardware
- Computer Software
- Consulting
- Financial Services
- High Tech

- Internet/New Media
- Investment Banking
- Investment Management
- Law
- Semiconductors
- Telecommunications
- Other

You'll find many interesting observations about the types of interview situations, types and examples of questions asked, and various problems encountered during the interview and with the company. The site also includes interviewing tips and salary reviews of companies.

Joyce Lain Kennedy   Job Interviews
dummies.com/resources/jobquestions/default.htm

This site catalogs over 1,000 sample job interview questions which may not have been included in syndicated columnist Joyce Lain Kennedy's best-selling job interview book, *Job Interviews for Dummies*.

MeetIT   **Job Interviews**
meetit.com

If you are an information technology specialist, this site should prove useful. It includes hundreds of sample questions employers and recruiters are most likely to ask. It also recommends positive responses as well as includes many interview tips on everything from telephone interviews to nonverbal behavior.

Interview Coach   **Job Interviews**
interviewcoach.com

This is one of several "Interview Coach" websites which charge fees for interview consultation services. Interview coach Carole Martin, who is <u>Monster.com</u>'s "Interview Expert," operates this website. It includes a free multiple-choice practice interview to test your ability to answer questions in the most positive manner possible. This sample is well worth reviewing for seeing alternative responses to some of the most frequently asked interview questions. Through this site you can purchase an interview workbook and hire Carole Martin to help you prepare for the job interview either by telephone or in person.

Salary and Compensation

Assuming you've been successful with your job interviews, the job offer and salary negotiations come next. Never negotiate salary until you have received a job offer. At this stage you need to conduct research on what you are worth and the various elements that should go into your compensation package *before* you talk about salary. Knowing what you are really worth in today's job market will give you an advantage when it's time to negotiate compensation.

Compensation is always one of those sensitive subjects. Since many people are taught not to talk about salaries, they often don't know what other people in comparable positions are making. Fortunately, the Internet includes a great deal of salary information which you can quickly access to determine your worth. The following websites are some of the best for accessing salary information and negotiation tips:

Salary.com	Salary Negotiations
salary.com	

If you want to know what other people are making in comparable positions, be sure to visit this website. Its "Salary Wizard" quickly gives you access to salary data for hundreds of positions in major metropolitan areas throughout the U.S. Just use the pull-down menus to select your job category and metropolitan area, or type in your zip code, and the site will give you salary ranges for the positions in its database. The site also includes salary news, salary advice, job listings, a resume database, and a jobs by email feature. Many of the websites featured in this book have a salary calculator section powered by Salary.com.

SalaryExpert.com	Salary Negotiations
salaryexpert.com	

This site includes free salary information on over 30,000 positions. Each report includes a position description, salary ranges, benefits, and other useful information. The site also includes salary information on more than 200 countries as well as other salary resources. Operated by Baker, Thomsen Associates, a compensation and benefits consulting firm.

JobStar.org	Salary Negotiations
jobstar.org	

Operated for libraries in California, JobStar pulls together numerous resources for assisting job seekers throughout California. It's especially noted for its compilation of over 300 general and profession-specific salary surveys which can be accessed through this site. Includes a "Salary I.Q." test, salary negotiation tips, and several salary-related articles (through a link with careerjournal.com).

Wageweb   Salary Negotiations
www.wageweb.com

This subscription-based site ($169-$219 per year) is designed for employers and HR professionals in search of compensation data on over 170 benchmark positions. Includes salary data on several professional positions, from finance to health care. You can review a few job descriptions and corresponding salary data on this site. Also includes frequently asked questions and links to HR websites.

Abbott-Langer   Salary Negotiations
abbott-langer.com

Abbott, Langer, and Associates, Inc. publishes several proprietary salary surveys on over 450 benchmark jobs. Covers jobs in information technology, marketing/sales, accounting, engineering, human resources, consulting, manufacturing, nonprofit, legal, and other fields. Most reports cost $295 each but you can view summary salary data on a few positions at no charge. The site also includes several useful HR articles.

Robert Half International   Salary Negotiations
www.rhii.com

With 330 offices in North America, Europe, and Australia, this is one of the world's largest staffing firms. It specializes in staffing temporary, full-time, and project professionals in the fields of accounting and finance, administrative support, information technology, law, advertising, marketing, and Web design. It publishes annual salary guides for several relevant positions. The guides are free upon request by completing the request form found in the "Resource Center." The accounting and finance guide can be downloaded in PDF format. This website also includes resources on resumes, cover letters, and interviews as well as links to other sites. The site also allows job seekers to browse job openings and submit resumes online.

Monster.com	**Salary Negotiations**
content.monster.com/salarylinks	
salarycenter.monster.com	

Like other sections of the huge Monster.com site, this one includes numerous linkages to other websites offering salary and compensation information as well as information on researching salaries, negotiations, benefits, evaluating offers, and salary comparables. Includes a salary/money bulletin board and links to Robert Half International's salary database.

SalarySource.com	**Salary Negotiations**
salarysource.com	

This site includes salary information on nearly 350 benchmark positions as well as salary tips. Can search by city. The site charges $29.95 for each salary inquiry. Includes several articles on compensation and job descriptions.

Other compensation-related sites worth visiting for addressing various aspects of the job negotiation process include:

- BenefitsLink — benefitslink.com
- BenefitNews.com — benefitnews.com
- Bureau of Labor Statistics — www.bls.gov
- CareerCity — careercity.com/content/salaries/links.asp
- CareerJournal — careerjournal.com
- CompensationLink — compensationlink.com

- CompGeo Online   claytonwallis.com/cxgonl.
                                                 html

- Employee Benefit
  Research Institute   ebri.org
- Homestore.com   homestore.com
                                                 homefair.com
- MyJobSearch   myjobsearch.com/
                                                 negotiating.html
- Quintessential Careers   quintcareers.com/salary_
                                                 negotiation.html
- Riley Guide   rileyguide.com/salguides.html
- SalariesReview.com   salariesreviews.com
- SalaryMaster   salarymaster.com
- Salary Surveys for
  Northwest Employers   salarysurveys.milliman.com
- Yahoo   careers.yahoo.com/careers/
                                                 salaries.html

For more information on how to integrate this Web-based salary information into your job search – including offline resources, sample salary negotiation dialogues, and compensation checklists – see our companion salary negotiations volume: ***Haldane's Best Salary Tips For Professionals*** (Impact Publications, 2001).

9

Relocation and Community Sites

A JOB OR CAREER CHANGE OFTEN MEANS MAKING A geographic move for a variety of personal and professional reasons. Whether you're planning to move to a nearby community, across country, or overseas, relocation will involve calculating new costs and projecting new opportunities. For many people, relocation is both stressful and liberating. When combined with a new job, it can energize one's career and life. Indeed, if you want to change your life, consider changing both your job and your community.

Relocation issues can arise at any time during your job search. As part of your initial planning, you may want to incorporate important lifestyle considerations in a job or career change. For example, what is your dream community – an ideal place you would love to live, work, and raise a family? Which communities are considered the best places in which to live and work? What do you need to do to target a job search campaign on such communities? When considering a job offer that involves relocation, you need to consider the economic implications of such a move. Who, for example, will handle the details of relocation? How much is your compensation package really worth in a community with a higher cost of living than in your current community? Answers to many of these and other relocation-relevant questions can be found on a variety of websites focusing on relocation issues.

Best Places to Live

Several publications periodically identify the 10, 50, 100, or 300 best places to live and work. Many of these studies are conducted and published annually. Most of these studies also are posted to websites. If you want to quickly survey the latest thinking on the best places to live, visit these websites:

- America's Best Online — americasbestonline.com/cities.htm
- ChooseToCruise — choosetocruise.com/americatwo.html
- Digital City — digitalcity.com/bestplacestolive
- Find Your Spot — findyourspot.com
- Kid Friendly Cities — kidfriendlycities.org/2001
- Money Magazine — money.com/money/depts/real_estate/bplive
- Real Estate Journal — homes.wsj.com/toolkit_res/bestplaces.html
- Sperling's BestPlaces — www.bestplaces.net
- School Report — theschoolreport.com

Great Places to Work

The following websites include lists, or links to other sites with such lists, of the best places to work in the United States:

- BestJobsUSA — bestjobsusa.com/sections/CAN-bestplaces2001
- EmploymentSpot — employmentspot.com/lists
- Forbes Magazine — forbes.com/lists
- Fortune Magazine — fortune.com (see "Fortune Lists")

- Great Place to Work — greatplacetowork.com/
  100best/100best.html
- Hoovers.com — hoovers.com/company/
  lists_best
- iVillage — ivillage.com/work
- JobStar Central — jobstar.org/hidden/bestcos.htm
- Quintessential Careers — quintcareers.com/best_
  places_to_work.html
- Working Woman — workingwoman.com

Community Access Sites

If you are interested in exploring various communities, be sure to visit these useful city sites which provide a wealth of information on each community:

- Boulevards — boulevards.com
- CitySearch — citysearch.com
- City Travel Guide — citytravelguide.com
- DigitalCity — digitalcity.com
- Insiders' Guides — insiders.com
- TOWD — www.towd.com
- USA City Link — usacitylink.com
- Yahoo — list.realestate.yahoo.com/
  re/neighborhood/main.html

Newspapers and magazines also provide useful information on the who, what, where, and when of communities, including job opportunities. For direct links to thousands of city newspapers and other local publications in North America and abroad, examine the following sites:

- Internet Public Library — ipl.org/reading/news
- NewsDirectory.com — newsdirectory.com
- NewspaperLinks — newspaperlinks.com
- Newspapers.com — www.newspapers.com

Useful Relocation Sites

Some of the most interesting, informative, and reassuring websites for job seekers are relocation sites. They provide access to different communities and address many personal and professional issues often taken for granted in one's current community.

The following sites are specifically designed to assist individuals with various aspects of relocation, from researching communities and calculating the local cost-of-living to finding housing, surveying schools, and identifying local cultural opportunities and community organizations and services.

Homestore.com	**Relocation**
homestore.com or **homefair.com**	

This is one of the most ubiquitous relocation sites appearing on employment websites. It's also one of the best sites for assisting individuals on just about every conceivable issue affecting relocation and transition. Indeed, this site usually powers the relocation sections of most employment websites. It includes information on several issues affecting relocation: cities, schools, crime, lifestyle, insurance, finance, employment, cost-of-living differences, planning, home ownership, professional movers, packing tips, storage, taxes, and moving to a new state. Its "Why – moving through this life transition made easy" section offers information on graduating, getting a job, getting married, raising children, getting promoted, emptying the nest, and retiring.

Virtual Relocation	**Relocation**
virtualrelocation.com	
monstermoving.com	

Part of the huge Monster.com website, this site is loaded with useful information on handling domestic and international relocation. Covers such relocation issues as finding a home, shopping for a mortgage rate, finding a mover, changing addresses, planning and managing a move, and living and shopping in a new community. Its international relocation section includes a visa help desk, relocation tools, country information, and key service providers (international moving and storage companies).

| **Relocation Central** | **Relocation** |
| **relocationcentral.com** | |

Although not immediately apparent, this site is rich with community-based information that you should include in any long-distance job search. Just select a city and you'll immediately access a huge database of local information on everything from apartments to the weather. The city profiles also include a local unemployment rate along with a list of the "Top Employers" in each community. The site includes numerous relocation tools, tips, checklists, and directories. Parents should find the education and school report sections for each community especially revealing.

| **Runzheimer International** | **Relocation** |
| **runzheimer.com** | |

This is one of the oldest and largest relocation companies that works with thousands of employers in relocating over 1 million employees each year. It is primarily designed for employers who use Runzheimer's services. Includes a two-location cost-of-living comparison service (fee-based) with a revealing sample report, which should give you a good idea of what you should be calculating when comparing relative cost-of-living differences between two communities. You'll need to include such considerations when figuring the comparable worth of a compensation package.

Job Relocation   Relocation
www.jobrelocation.com

Operated by salesman-realtor-Web designer-relocation special-ist Steve Levine, this commercial site is primarily designed for executive-level candidates and recruiters who need important relocation information before accepting or rejecting a job offer. While this site includes fee-based services, it also includes several free services and tools: cost-of-living reports, home-selling assistance, relocation package, cost-of-living counseling, and personalized recruiter and job candidate consultations. Includes a few relocation articles and linkages.

Homescape   Relocation
homescape.com

If you're primarily interested in finding and financing housing, this site can provide assistance. Its database includes over 900,000 homes in 25,000 cities. The site allows users to search for mortgage rates, apply for loans, find apartments, locate a real estate agent, sell a home, and locate a moving company or truck rental firm.

Several other websites also provide useful relocation information on domestic and international relocation. Check out the following sites for everything from tips on changing your address, ordering moving supplies, and connecting your utilities (www.usps.gov/moversnet) to handling the whole relocation process, from A to Z, both domestically and internationally (insiders.com/relocation):

- 123Relocation.com   relo-usa.com
- Employee Relocation Council   erc.org
- GMAC Relocation Services   gmac-relocation.com
- Insiders' Guide   insiders.com/relocation
- MoversNet   www.usps.gov/moversnet

- Moving.com   moving.com
- MovingCost.com   movingprices.com
- Relocate-America   relocate-america.com
- Relocation-net.com   www.relocation-net.com
- The Wall Street Journal   homes.wsj.com

If a community move enters into your job search plans, make sure you visit several of the websites outlined in this chapter. These are some of the most revealing websites. Indeed, one of the great values of the Internet is its wealth of searchable community-based information. This information can help job seekers with everything from locating jobs and employers to calculating cost-of-living and making a physical move.

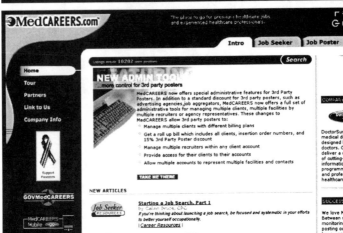

10

Industry and Occupational Sites

O NE OF THE BEST KEPT SECRETS ON THE INTERNET for job seekers is the wealth of specialty employment websites. Known as boutique or niche sites, they focus on a single industry or occupation. In contrast to the mega employment sites featured in Chapter 6, which try to appeal to all employers, recruiters, and job seekers, the sites featured in this chapter are targeted toward the skills and interests of specific occupational groups and professions. Many of these sites are proving to be more effective for employers and job seekers than the mega employment sites. Indeed, the trend is for more and more employers and job seekers to use these sites for connecting with each other.

Finding the Perfect Site

Specialty employment websites can be easily found by using search engines, gateway websites, and professional associations. As outlined in Chapter 3, the following search engines should prove useful in locating such sites:

- Google   google.com
- 1-Page Multi Search   bjorgul.com
- Search IQ   searchiq.com
- All Search Engines   allsearchengines.com
- GoGettem   gogettem.com

Useful gateway sites for locating specialty employment websites include the following:

- AIRS Directory   airsdirectory.com/jobboards
- Quintessential Careers   quintcareers.com
- The Riley Guide   rileyguide.com

Some of the best specialty employment websites are operated by professional associations. The major gateway sites for locating appropriate associations are:

- Assocations on the Net   ipl.org/ref/AON
- AssociationCentral   associationcentral.com
- American Society of
  Association Executives   www.asaenet.org

Academia and Education

If you are interested in teaching and related education jobs, the following websites are some of the best for locating opportunities in K-12 and higher education:

- Academic360.com   academic360.com
- Chronicle of Higher
  Education   chronicle.com/jobs
- Higher Education Jobs   higheredjobs.com
- Education America Network   educationamerica.net
- K-12Jobs   k12jobs.com
- Academic Employment
  Network   Academploy.com

Other useful sites for educators include the following:

- Academic Careers Online   academiccareers.com
- Academic Position Network   apnjobs.com
- Carney Sandoe & Associates   csa-teach.com
- C-collegeJobs.com   ccollegejobs.com
- Ed-U-Link   edulink.com
- Education Jobs   nationjob.com/education
- EducationJobs.com   educationjobs.com
- Education World   educationworld.com/jobs
- ESLworldwide.com   eslworldwide.com
- iTeachNet (international)   iteachnet.com
- Jobsinschools.com   jobsinschools.com
- National Teacher Recruitment Clearinghouse   recruitingteachers.org
- Private School Jobs   privateschooljobs.com
- School Staff   schoolstaff.com
- Teacher Job Links   geocities.com/athens/forum/2080
- Teacherjobsite.com   www.teacherjobsite.com
- Teachers Employment Network   teachingjobs.com
- TeachersNet   teachers.net/jobs
- Teacher's Planet.com   teachersplanet.com
- Teachers @ Work   teachersatwork.com
- Teachers-Teachers.com   teachers-teachers.com
- Teaching Jobs Overseas   joyjobs.com
- TeachWave   teachwave.com
- TEFLnetJobs   tefl.net/jobs
- TESOL JobFinder   tesol.org/careers
- The International Educator   tieonline.com
- USTeach.com   usteach.com
- WantToTeach.com   www.wanttoteach.com
- Women in Higher Education   wihe.com/jobs

Architecture

If you work in the architectural field, be sure to visit these two popular websites:

- Architect Jobs   architectjobs.com
- Architect Search   archsearch.com
                          architect-placement.com

Since architecture-related jobs are often found on construction websites, be sure to visit several of the sites outlined under the construction section. The following websites also provide numerous opportunities for achitects:

- A/E/C JobBank   aecjobbank.com
- Computer Architect Jobs www.computerarchitect
                          jobs.com
- Craig's List   craigslist.org
- Just Architect Jobs   justarchitectjobs.com
- Landscape Architects   landscapearchitects.org

Arts, Entertainment, and Media

If you are interested in exploring job and career opportunities in the arts, entertainment, and media industries, be sure to check out these websites. Most include specialized job postings and resume databases:

- Entertainment Careers   entertainmentcareers.net
- ShowBizJobs.com   showbizjobs.com
- HollywoodWeb   hollywoodweb.com
- Art Job Online   artjob.org

These websites also include useful employment information for individuals interested in the fields of arts, entertainment, and media:

- 440 International (Radio) 440int.com
- AM/FM Jobs   amfmjobs.com
- Aquent   portfolio.skill.com
- ArtHire   arthire.com
- Artist Resource   www.artistresource.org/
                          jobs.htm
- Arts Resume Resources   wwar.com/employment-
                          resume

- ArtSource   artsource.com
- Entertainment Job Search   dnaproductions.com/jobs.
                                               htm
- Medialine   www.medialine.com
- Media Jobz   mediajobz.com
- MediaRecruiter   mediarecruiter.com
- National Association of
  Broadcasters Career Center   nab.org/bcc
- Playbill Online   playbill.com/cgi-bin/plb/
                                               jobs?cmd=search
- Radio Online   radioonline.com
- Talent Works   talentworks.com
- Temp Art   tempart.com
- TVandRadioJobs.com   tvandradiojobs.com
- TVJobs.com   tvjobs.com

Aviation and Airline Industry

The aviation and airline industry offers thousands of professional opportunities for enterprising job seekers. The following websites represent some of the best sites for exploring such opportunities. Many of them charge a monthly or yearly membership fee to access a site's job postings or use its resume database:

- Airline Career.com   airlinecareer.com
- Aviation Jobs Online   www.aviationjobsonline.com
- Airline Employment
  Assistance Corps and
  AV Jobs Worldwide   avjobs.com

From pilots to ground crew, the following employment websites also offer a wealth of online opportunities for individuals in the aviation and airline industry:

- Airline Employee
  Placement Service   aeps.com
- Airline Job Site   airlinejobsite.com
- Airport Job Hub   airportjobhub.com

- Airport Job Kiosk — airportjobkiosk.com
- Aviation Communication — flightinfo.com
- Aviation Job Search — www.aviationjobsearch.com
- Aviation World Services — aviationworldservices.com/employ.htm
- AviationNet — aviationnet.com
- AvScholars — avscholars.com
- Be a Pilot — beapilot.com
- Find a Pilot — findapilot.com
- Flight Deck Recruitment — www.flightdeckrecruitment.com
- Flightline — flightline.com
- Flying Talent — www.flyingtalent.com
- Helicopter Employment — avemployment.com
- Jet Careers — jetcareers.com
- Jet-Jobs — jet-jobs.com
- Jobs in Aviation — jobsinaviation.com
- Pilots Wanted — pilotswanted.com
- Traveljobz.net — traveljobz.net

Business

Many of the employment websites featured in Chapter 7 relate to job and career opportunities in a variety of business fields. Indeed, many of those sites include channels which classify jobs into numerous occupational and professional channels. At the same time, hundreds of websites focus on particular business fields. Some of the best such sites include:

- Careers in Business — careers-in-business.com
- Bank Jobs — bankjobs.com
- Benefitslink.com — benefitslink.com/jobs/index.shtml
- Telecom Careers — telecomcareers.net
- Accountant Jobs — accountantjobs.com
- Financial Jobs — www.financialjobs.com
- Jobs4Sales — jobs4sales.com

Computers and Information Technology

The computer and information technology fields have traditionally been major users of the Internet for connecting job seekers with employers and recruiters. These fields further break down into highly specialized employment websites focused on specific applications, such as Oracle and UNIX, new media, web design, telecom, and particular hardware and software programs. Some of the best computer and IT employment sites include the following:

- DICE   dice.com
- Computer Jobs   computerjobs.com
- IT Careers.com   itcareers.com
- Computer Work   computerwork.com
- American Jobs   americanjobs.com

Other computer and IT employment websites worth visiting include:

- AwesomeTechs.com   awesometechs.com
- Brainbench   brainbench.com
- Brainpower   brainpower.com
- Brainbuzz   brainbuzz.com
- Brassring (see Chapter 7)   brassring.com
- CareerShopIT   it.careershop.com
- CareerWeb (see Chapter 7)   careerweb.com
- ComputerScience Jobs   computersciencejobs.com
- Craig's List   craigslist.org
- DatabaseJobs.com   databasejobs.com
- Hire Strategy   hirestrategy.com
- Hot Tech Careers   www.hottechcareers.com
- IT Talent   ittalent.com
- Jobs4IT   jobs4it.com
- JustASPJobs   justaspjobs.com
- Operation IT   operationit.com
- Search Database   searchdatabase.com
- Techies.com   techies.com

Construction

The fields of architecture, construction, and engineering are closely related. Many of the jobs appearing on architecture and engineering web sites also appear on construction employment websites. If you consider your occupational field more directly related to construction, be sure to visit these two top construction websites:

- Construction Jobs   constructionjobs.com
- Construction Job Store   constructionjobstore.com

Other useful employment websites with a disproportionate number of construction-related jobs include:

- Architect Jobs   architectjobs.com
- Careers in Construction   careersinconstruction.com
- Carpenter Jobs   carpenterjobs.com
- Construction Gigs   constructiongigs.com
- Construction Managers Job   constructionmanagerjob.com
- Construction Work Jobs   constructionworkjobs.com
- Contract Professionals   contractprofessionals.net
- Craft Hotline   crafthotline.com
- Electrician Jobs   electricianjobs.com
- Engineer Employment   engineeremployment.com
- Estimator Jobs   estimatorjobs.com
- iHire Construction   ihireconstruction.com
- Jobsite   www.jobsite.com
- Newhome Sales Jobs   newhomesalesjobs.com
- Plumber Jobs   plumberjobs.com
- Project Manager Jobs   projectmanagerjobs.com
- Trade Jobs Online   www.tradejobsonline.com

Engineering

Engineers belong to a wide range of engineering specialty fields. These websites are two of the best employment sites designed specifically for engineers:

- EngineeringJobs   www.engineeringjobs.com
- Engineer Employment   www.engineeringemployment.
                                    com

Engineers should also visit the following engineering websites for employment information and opportunities:

- Application-engineer-jobs   www.application-engineer-
                                jobs.com
- Biomedical Engineer   biomedicalengineer.com
- Chemical Engineer   chemicalengineer.com
- Chemical Engineer Jobs   www.chemicalengineer
                                jobs.com
- Civil Engineer Jobs   civilengineerjobs.com
- Contract Engineering   contractengineering.com
- Craig's List   craigslist.com
- Engineering-jobs-here   engineering-jobs-here.com
- Environmental Engineer   environmentalengineer.com
- Industrial Engineer   industrialengineer.com
- Manufacturing Engineer   manufacturingengineer.com
- Mechanical Engineer   mechanicalengineer.com
- Network Engineer   networkengineer.com
- Petroleum Engineer   petroleumengineer.com
- Process Engineer Jobs   processengineerjobs.com
- Sales Engineer   salesengineer.com
- Semiconductor Engineer   semiconductorengineer.com
- Software Engineer   softwareengineer.com

Health Care and Medicine

Health care and medicine constitute a huge and rapidly growing industry. Numerous specialized employment websites, from professional associations to recruiters, focus on recruiting for a wide range of health care positions and fields, such as physician, nurse, radiology, dental, allied health, and emergency medicine. Some of the top health care websites include:

- Absolutely Health Care   healthcarejobsusa.com
- Monster Healthcare   healthcare.monster.com

- MedHunters.com   medhunters.com
- MedCAREERS   www.medcareers.com

You should also include several of the following health-related websites in your job search:

- 4 MD Jobs.com   4mdjobs.com
- 4 Nursing Jobs.Com   4nursingjobs.com
- Allied Health Employment   gvpub.com
- Community Health Systems   www.chs.net
- CompHealth   comphealth.com
- Dentist Jobs   dentistjobs.com
- DentSearch   dentsearch.com
- DocJob.com   docjob.com
- Echo-Web   echocareers.com
- e-Dental   e-dental.com
- EmployMED   employmed.com
- GovMedCareers   govmedcareers.com
- Health Care Jobs Online   hcjobsonline.com
- Health Care Recruiters   hcrecruiters.com
- Healthcare Careers Online   healthcareers.com
- Health Care Jobs (book)   healthcarejobs.org
- Health Care Job Store   healthcarejobstore.com
- Health Care Recruitment   healthcareers-online.com
- Health Care Source   healthcaresource.com
- Health Care Talents   www.healthcaretalents.com
- Health Care Works   healthcareworks.org
- Health CareerWeb   healthcareerweb.com
- Health Jobsite.com   www.healthjobsite.com
- Healthlinks.net   www.healthlinks.net
- Health Network USA   www.hnusa.com
- Health Opps   healthopps.com
- HIPjobs.net   HIPjobs.net
- Hospitalhub.com   hospitalhub.com
- Hospital Jobs Online   hospitaljobsonline.com
- Hospital Jobs USA   hospitaljobsusa.com
- iHireNursing   ihirenursing.com
- iHirePhysicians.com   ihirephysicians.com

- Job Health   jobhealth.net
- Job Health Careers   jobhealthcareers.net
- Jobscience   jobscience.com
- MD Direct.com   mddirect.com
- MDJobSite.com   mdjobsite.com
- Med Bulletin   medbulletin.com
- Med Options   medoptions.com
- Medical Office Resources   mor-online.com
- Medical-Posts.com   medical-posts.com
- Medical Sales Jobs   medicalsalesjobs.com
- Medimorphus.com   medimorphus.com
- Medjump   medjump.com
- MedZilla   medzilla.com
- Nursejobz   nursejobz.com
- Nurse-Recruiter.com   nurse-recruiter.com
- Nursing Spectrum   nursingspectrum.com
- Pharmaceutical Rep Jobs   pharmaceuticalrepjobs.com
- PhysicianBoard   physicianboard.com
- Physician Employment   physicianemployment.com
- Physician Finders   www.physicianfinders.com
- Practice Choice   practicechoice.com
- RTJobs.com   rtjobs.com
- Ultrasoundjobs.com   ultrasoundjobs.com
- Vital Careers   vitalcareers.com

Hospitality and Travel

Hospitality and travel represent a global industry that employs millions of individuals in hotels, resorts, restaurants, amusement parks, convention centers, spas, travel agencies, tourist promotion offices, car rental companies, cruise lines, clubs, and casinos. This highly segmented industry is also highly wired when it comes to job opportunities. Most players in this industry have their own websites. Some of major hospitality and travel employment websites include:

- Hospitality Adventures   hospitalityadventures.com
- Hospitality Careers Online hcareers.com
- Job Monkey.com   jobmonkey.com

Also, be sure to check out many of the following websites that focus on particular employment sectors within the hospitality and travel industry:

- Action Jobs — actionjobs.com
- Casino Careers Online — casinocareers.com
- Chef Job — chefjob.com
- Chef Jobs Network — chefjobsnetwork.com
- Chefs on the Net — chefnet.com
- Cool Works — coolworks.com
- e-Hospitality.com — e-hospitality.com
- Entree Job Bank — entreejobbank.com
- Escoffier.com — escoffier.com
- Food Industry Jobs.com — foodindustryjobs.com
- Food Management Search — foodmanagementsearch.com
- Foodservice Central — foodservicecentral.com
- Food Service.com — foodservice.com
- Food Smack — foodsmack.com
- Harrison Business Group — harrisonbusinessgroup.com
- Hospitality Careers — www.hospitalitycareers.net
- Hospitality Financial and Technology Professionals — iaha.org
- Hospitality Jobs Online — hotel-jobs.com
- Hospitality Link — hospitalitylink.com
- Hospitality Net — hospitalitynet.org
- Hospitality Online — hospitalityonline.com
- Hotel Job Resource — hoteljobresource.com
- Hoteljobs.com — hoteljobs.com
- Hotel Jobs Network — hoteljobsnetwork.com
- Hotel Online Classifieds — hotel-online.com
- Hotel Resource — hotelresource.com
- Hotels Hiring Online — hotels.hiringonline.com
- iHire Hospitality — ihirehospitality.com
- iHire Hospitality Services — ihirehospitalityservices.com
- International Seafarers — jobxchange.com
- Jobs in Paradise — jobsinparadise.com
- Meeting Jobs — meetingjobs.com

- Meeting Professionals International	www.mpiweb.org/resources/jobs
- Outdoor Network	outdoornetwork.com
- Resort Jobs	resortjobs.com
- Resort Recruitment	resortrecruitment.com.au
- Restaurant Manager.net	restaurantmanager.net
- Restaurant Managers.Com	restaurantmanagers.com
- SE Hospitality	sehospitality.net
- Ship Center.com	shipcenter.com
- SkiingtheNet.com	skiingthenet.com
- Ski Resort Jobs	skiresortjobs.com
- Spa Jobs	spajobs.com
- Travel Jobs	traveljobs.com
- Traveljobz.net	traveljobz.net
- Workamper.com	workamper.com
- Working Vacation	theworkingvacation.com

Law

From paralegals to attorneys, the Internet has become a center for several law-related employment websites. Some of the best employment websites, which include resume databases and job postings for a wide range of legal professionals, include:

- Legalstaff	legalstaff.com
- Attorney Jobs Online	attorneyjobsonline.com
- Law.com CareerCenter	lawjobs.com

Other useful legal websites include:

- 411 Legal Info	411legalinfo.com/JOBS
- Attorney Job Store	attorneyjobstore.com
- AttorneyJobs.com	www.attorneyjobs.com
- Corporate Attorney Jobs	corporateattorneyjobs.com
- CounselHounds.com	counselhounds.com
- Counsel.net	counsel.net
- Craig's List	craigslist.com
- eAttorney	eattorney.com

- Emplawyer.net   emplawyernet.com
- Environmentalattorneyjobs   environmentalattorney
                                   jobs.com
- FindLaw Career Center   careers.findlaw.com
- Find Law Job.com   findlawjob.com
- Global Law Jobs   paralegal.i12.com
- iHire Legal   ihirelegal.com
- Jobs.LawInfo.com   jobs.lawinfo.com
- Juris Resources.com   jurisresources.com
- LawGuru.com   lawguru.com
- LawListings.com   lawlistings.com
- Law Match   lawmatch.com
- LawyersweeklyJobs.com   lawyersweeklyjobs.com
- LegalCV.com (UK)   legalcv.com
- Legal Employment   legalemploy.com
- LegalHire.com   legalhire.com
- Legal Job Store   legaljobstore.com
- Litigation Attorney Jobs   litigationattorneyjobs.com
- NationJob Network   nationjob.com/legal
- Paralegal.com   paralegal.com
- Paralegal-Jobs.com   paralegal-jobs.com
                                   paralegalclassifieds.com
- Paralegals.org   paralegals.org
- US Legal Jobs   uslegaljobs.com

Science

The scientific community includes numerous professional fields, with biology, chemistry, and geology having a significant online presence. Three of the best employment websites for a wide range of scientists include:

- BioView   bioview.com
- Science Careers   recruit.sciencemag.org
- JobSpectrum.org   jobspectrum.org

Other useful specialty employment websites designed for different scientific communities include:

- Air Weather Association   airweaassn.org/jobs.htm
- Bio Online   career.bio.com
- ChemCenter   acs.org/careers/employer/
                             index.html
- Chemical Online   chemicalonline.com
- ChemistryJobs.com   www.chemistryjobs.com
- ChemJobs.net   chemjobs.net
- Earthworks   earthworks-jobs.com
- GeoJobs International   geojobs.com
- GeoSearch   geosearch.com
- GeoTechJobs   geotechjobs.com
- JobScience.com   jobscience.com
- Jobs4Scientists   www.ajobs4scientists.com
- NatureJobs   nature.com/naturejobs
- ScienceOnline   recruit.sciencemag.org
- SciJobs.org   scijobs.org
- WeatherJobs.com   weatherjobs.com

Sports and Recreation

Sports and recreation jobs are well represented on several specialty employment websites that cover everything from golf, coaching, and summer camps to skiing, tennis, racing, and sports medicine. Three of the best such websites include:

- JobsinSports.com   jobsinsports.com
- CoolWorks.com   coolworks.com
- GolfingCareers   golfingcareers.com

Several other sports- and recreation-related employment sites offer a large number of opportunities:

- ActionJobs.com   actionjobs.com
- Camp Channel   campchannel.com/campjobs
- Camp Jobs   campjobs.com
- Camp Staff   campstaff.com

- C.O.A.C.H. — coachhelp.com/exe-bin/jsearch.cfm
- Coaching Jobs — coachingjobs.com
- Executive Sports Placement — prosportsjobs.com
- Gameops.com — gameops.com/tools/jobs.htm
- GolfSurfin — golfsurfin.com
- Great Summer Jobs — gsj.petersons.com
- JobMonkey — jobmonkey.com
- Monster Sports Jobs/ESPN — espn.monster.com
- Mountain Jobs — mountainjobs.com
- My Summers — mysummers.com
- NCAA Online — ncaa.org/employment.html
- OnlineSports.com — onlinesports.com
- Outdoor JobNet — outdoornetwork.com/jobnetdb/index.html
- Racing Jobs — racingjobs.com
- SkiingtheNet.com — skiingthenet.com
- Ski Resort Jobs — skiresortjobs.com
- Sports Business — sportsbusiness.about.com/cs/employment
- Sports Careers — 1andall-sportsjobs.com
- Sports Employment — sportsemployment.com
- Sports Jobs For Women — sportsjobsforwomen.com
- Sports Medicine — sportsmedicinejobs.com
- Sports Work — sportswork.com
- Sports Workers — sportsworkers.com
- TeamJobs.com — teamjobs.com
- Tennis Jobs — tennisjobs.com
- Title 9 Sports — title9sports.com/jobs.html
- Women's Sports Careers — womensportsjobs.com
- Work in Sports — workinsports.com

Whatever your occupational specialty, chances are you will find employment websites that specialize in your area of expertise. If you have difficulty locating websites related to your occupational interests through the standard directories and search engines, always check with a relevant professional association to see if it sponsors online employment services related to your interests.

11

Job Seeker Sites

HUNDREDS OF EMPLOYMENT WEBSITES ALSO ARE designed for special categories of job seekers. Responding to special needs, these websites cut across standard occupational fields. If, for example, you are an executive, student, veteran, female, minority, or a freelancer, you will find several websites responsive to your employment interests. If your employment interests are less oriented toward business and more focused toward government agencies, nonprofit organizations, and the international arena, you'll find several employment websites designed for these particular employment arenas.

Executives and $100,000+ Jobs

Most employment websites disproportionately represent jobs that pay in the range of $25,000 to $70,000. If you are an executive-level candidate, or someone who anticipates making over $100,000 a year, you may find most general websites to be less than rewarding for your efforts. Instead, you may decide it's best to target your job search toward executive search firms and headhunters who claim to have an "inside track" on the hidden job market that seeks executive-level talent.

The executive-level job market has its own particular structure with segments that may or may not involve the use of the Internet. One way to quickly gain access to the major players in this hidden job market is to use resume blasting services, such as <u>Resumezapper.com</u>, which we discussed in Chapter 5. Another way is to contact appropriate executive recruiters directly by sending them a copy of your resume and a cover letter. The best online source for identifying executive recruiters by occupational specialty (14 categories), is **Oya's Directory of Recruiters** site:

<u>i-recruit.com</u>

Several websites also specialize in providing employment assistance to executive-level candidates. Many of these sites are operated by executive search firms in search of uniquely qualified talent to market to their high-end clients. In contrast to other employment websites, which charge employers fees to post jobs and search resume databases, some of these sites charge candidates monthly or yearly fees to use their job search services. Employers and headhunters are often given free access to the site's resume database. The following executive-level job sites are free to job seekers:

- **6 Figure Jobs**   <u>sixfigurejobs.com</u>
- **Chief Monster.com**   <u>my.chief.monster.com</u>
- **Management Recruiters International**   <u>brilliantpeople.com</u>
- **Recruiters Online Network**   <u>recruitersonline.com</u>

These sites charge job seekers membership fees to access their online executive services:

- **ExecuNet**   <u>execunet.com</u>
- **ExecutivesOnly**   <u>executivesonly.com</u>
- **Netshare**   <u>netshare.com</u>

College Graduates

If you are a college student or recent graduate, you'll find numerous websites designed to assist you with your job search as well as your transition from education to the work world. More so than many of the mega employment sites featured in Chapter 5, these specialty sites include many useful job search tools, from self-assessment to interview and salary negotiation tips, as well as internship and education opportunities to assist graduates with their job search and career development. At the same time, many of the mega employment websites, such as Monster.com (jobtrak.com) and Careerbuilder.com, (college.careerbuilder.com), include special sections designed specifically for college students and recent graduates. Most college-oriented websites also include job postings and resume databases which tend to focus on entry-level positions.

If you are a college student or recent graduate first entering or re-entering the job market, be sure to check out these four major websites for college students:

- CampusCareerCenter   campuscareercenter.com
- Job Web   www.jobweb.com
- JobTrak   jobtrak.com
- CollegeJobs.com   www.collegejobs.com

The following websites also provide a wealth of online employment information and services for college students and recent graduates:

- 123Intern.com   123intern.com
- AboutJobs.com   aboutjobs.com
- AfterCollege.com   aftercollege.com
- Black Collegian   blackcollegian.com
- BrassRing Campus   brassringcampus.com
- CareerBuilder   college.careerbuilder.com
- CcollegeJobs.com   ccollegejobs.com
- College Central Network collegecentral.com
- College Grad Job Hunter collegegrad.com
- Collegejournal.com   collegejournal.com
- College News   collegenews.com/jobs.htm

- College Recruiter   collegerecruiter.com
- EmployU.com   employu.com
- Entryleveljobstore.com   entryleveljobstore.com
- eProNet   www.epronet.com
- EnviroLink Network   envirolink.netforchange.com
- Experience.com   experience.com
- Graduating Engineer Online   graduatingengineer.com
- InternJobs.com   internjobs.com
- InternshipPrograms.com   internshipprograms.com
- Internweb.com   www.internweb.com
- JobDirect.com   jobdirect.com
- JobMonkey.com   jobmonkey.com
- Kaplan, Inc.   kaplan.com
- NAGPS Internet Job Bank   nagps.org/Mailing-List.asp?
                               target=job-bank

Military and Veterans

If you are one of the 260,000 members of the U.S. military who leave the service each year for the civilian sector, or if you are a veteran in search of a new job, you should visit several military transition and veteran sites designed specifically for individuals with your background. These sites tend to attract military-friendly employers, many of which are defense contractors, who are seeking individuals with military experience. The following military transition and veteran sites include job postings and resume databases along with job search tools:

- Corporate Gray Online   www.greentogray.com
- VetJobs.com   vetjobs.com
- The Destiny Group   destinygroup.com
- TAOnline   taonline.com

Other useful websites for transitioning military personnel and veterans include these sites:

- Army Times   armytimes.com
- Armed Forces.com   armedforces.com
- Bradley-Morris.com   bradley-morris.com

- Cameron-Brooks cameron-brooks.com
- IntelligenceCareers.com intelligencecareers.com
- JMO Jobs www.jmojobs.com
- Lucas Group lucascareers.com/general/ military
- Mil2Civ.com mil2civ.com
- MilitaryCity.com militarycity.com
- Military.com military.com
- MilitaryHire.com militaryhire.com
- Military Outplacement Post midwestmilitary.com
- Military Partners militarypartners.com
- Military Transition militarytransition.com
- Military Transition Group careercommandpost.com
- Monster.com content.monster.com/military
- Military Overseas Recruiting Events, Inc. morejobfairs.net
- Non Commission Officers Association (NCOA) ncoausa.org
- Orion International www.orion-careernetwork. com
- TekSystems.com www.teksystems.com
- The Retired Officers Association (TROA) www.troa.org/tops
- Veteran Net veteran.net
- VeteransWorld.com www.veteransworld.com
- Vets4Hire vets4hire.com

Women

Several websites also specialize on providing employment assistance for women. Many of these sites, as discussed in Chapter 6, focus on networking and mentoring for women and are organized by occupational specialty and/or professional association. For example, many women's organizations focusing on construction, business, education, and technology operate their own specialty employment websites to assist women in finding jobs and managing their careers. The following websites should be of special interest to professional women in search of employment information and services in their respective fields:

- American Society of
  Women Accountants   aswa.org
- Association of Women
  in Mathematics   awm-math.org
- Association for Women
  in Sports Media   awsmonline.org
- Society of Women Engineers swe.org
- Women in Communication   womcom.org
- Women in Higher Education   wihe.com
- Women in Technology
  International   www.witi.com

The following websites specialize in providing job information and services to women in a variety of professional fields:

- iVillage   ivillage.com
- Career-Intelligence.com   career-intelligence.com
- CareerWomen   careerwomen.com
- Womans-Work   womans-work.com

Many of these same sites put special emphasis on assessment and testing as well as focus on family and workplace issues affecting the career development of women.

Several other websites also provide useful employment information and services for women:

- CareerWoman2000   careerwoman2000.com
- ClassifiedsForWomen   classifiedsforwomen.com
- Digital Women   digital-women.com/work.htm
- Feminist Majority
  Foundation Online   feminist.org
- Herwebbiz.com   herwebbiz.com
- Jobs4Women   jobs4women.com
- Msmoney.com   msmoney.com
- Women.com   women.com
- WomenInfoline.com   www.womeninfoline.com/
                             careers
- Womensforum.com   womensforum.com

- WomensJobSite.com   www.womensjobsite.com
- Women Sports Careers   womensportscareers.com
    womensportsjobs.com
- WomenWork.com   womenwork.com

Minorities and Diversity

If you are associated with a distinct minority or diversity group (race, ethnicity, religion, sexual orientation, age, citizenship, disability), you should find special websites designed for you. Many of these sites include employment information and services. Three of the best minority and diversity sites include:

- LatPro (Spanish/ Portuguese)   latpro.com
- Hire Diversity.com   hirediversity.com
- DiversityLink.com   diversitylink.com

Several other minority and diversity sites also are worth visiting for employment information and services:

- Africareers.com   africareers.com
- Asia-Net.com   asia-net.com
- Asia-Jobs.com   asia-jobs.com
- Asian Careers.com   www.asiancareers.com
- Best Diversity Employers   bestdiversityemployers.com
- Bilingual-Jobs   bilingual-jobs.com
- Black Collegian   blackcollegian.com
- Blackenterprise.com   blackenterprise.com
- Black Voices   new.blackvoices.com
- CareerMoves (Jewish)   www.jvsjobs.org
- ChristiaNet (Religious)   christianet.com/christianjobs
- ChristianJobs (Religious)   christianjobs.com
- CVLatino (Hispanic)   cvlatino.com
- Diversity Job Network   diversityjobnetwork.com
- Diversity Recruiting   diversityrecruiting.com
- Diversity Search.com   diversitysearch.com
- DiversiLink (Hispanic)   diversilink.com

- Diversity Employment — diversityemployment.com
- EOP Online — eop.com
- Gaywork.com (Gays) — gaywork.com
- Global Mission (Religious) — globalmission.org
- HireDiversity — hirediversity.com
- HispaniaNet.com (Hispanic) — hispanianet.com
- Hispanic Online Cyber Career Center — hispaniconline.com
- IMdiversity.com — imdiversity.com
- Jewishcampstaff.com (Jewish) — jewishcampstaff.com
- JobCentro (Hispanic) — jobcentro.com
- JobLatino (Hispanic) — joblatino.com
- LatinoWeb.com (Hispanic) — latinoweb.com
- MBXonline — mbxonline.com
- Ministry Connect (Religious) — ministryconnect.org
- MinistryJobs (Religious) — ministryjobs.com
- MinistrySearch.com — ministrysearch.com
- MinorityCareer.Com — www.minoritycareer.com
- MinorityNurse.com — minoritynurse.com
- Multicultural Advantage — tmaonline.net
- NativeAmericanJobs.com — nativeamericanjobs.com
- ProGayJobs.com (Gays) — progayjobs.com
- Saludos Hispanos (Hispanic) — saludoshispanos.com
- TodoLatino (Hispanic) — todolatino.com
- NativeJobs (Native-Americans) — nativejobs.com
- VisaJobs (Immigrants) — visajobs.com
- Youth Specialties (Religious) — youthspecialties.com
- WorkplaceDiversity.com — www.workplacediversity.com

People With Disabilities

If you have a particular disability that affects your work, you may want to explore several websites that increasingly focus on the career concerns of people with disabilities. In fact, studies show that most people will at some time go through a period of disability that affects their work. Over 50 million workers in the U.S. have some form of disability that relates to their work and their particular occupational choices. The following websites may be of some assistance, although many of them tend to focus more on providing information about disabilities, benefits, and training rather than on linking disabled job seekers to employers:

- State Vocational and Rehabilitation Agencies — trfn.clpgh.org/srac/state-vr.html
- Job Accommodation Network — www.jan.wvu.edu
- Job Access — jobaccess.org
- Disabled Person — www.disabledperson.com

The following websites also provide useful employment information and services to people with disabilities:

- Able to Work — abletowork.org
- Act-Together — geocities.com/CapitolHill/5975
- American Association of People With Disabilities — www.aapd-dc.org
- Careers On-Line — disserv3.stu.umn.edu/COL/index.html
- Challenge 2000 — www2.interaccess.com/netown/eeo/eeoempl.htm
- Choice Employment — choiceemployment.com
- Davjobs.com — davjobs.com
- Department of Labor — www.dol.gov/dol/odep/public/joblinks.htm
- EOP.com — eop.com/mag-cd.html
- Federal Jobs — federaljobs.net/disabled.htm
- Handiwork Online — handiworkonline.com
- New Mobility — newmobility.com
- The Work Site (SSA) — wwssa.gov/work/index2.html
- Training Resource Network — trninc.com
- WorkSupport — www.worksupport.com

Government and Law Enforcement

More than 20 million U.S. citizens, or nearly 15 percent of the total workforce, are employed by federal, state, or local governments. While most government agencies have their own websites, which may include employment information, several other websites specialize in aggregating government job listings into one-stop government employment sites. If you are interested in a federal government job or one in law enforcement, you should find these three websites especially helpful in conducting a government-related job search:

- USA Jobs   www.usajobs.opm.gov
- FederalJobsCentral   fedjobs.com
- Lawenforcementjob.com   lawenforcementjob.com

Several other websites focus on jobs at various levels of government:

- Careers in Government   careersingovernment.com
- Careers in Law Enforcement   lejobs.com
- Classified Employment
  Web Site   yourinfosource.com/CLEWS
- Cop Career.com   copcareer.com
- Corrections.com   database.corrections.com/
                                career
- Federal Jobs Digest   jobsfed.com
- Federal Jobs Net   federaljobs.net
- FederalJobSearch   federaljobsearch.com
- Federal Times   federaltimes.com
- FedGate   fedgate.org
- FedWorld.gov   www.fedworld.gov
- FirstGov   firstgov.gov
- GovernmentJobs.com   governmentjobs.com
- Govjobs.com   govjobs.com
                                govtjob.net
- Jobs4PublicSector (Europe)   jobs4publicsector.com
- Law Enforcement Job   lawenforcementjob.com
- Law Enforcement Jobs   lawenforcementjobs.com

- Officer.com   officer.com
- PoliceCareer.com   policecareer.com
- PSE-NET.com   PSE-NET.com
- StateJobs.com   statejobs.com
- United Nations   unsystem.org
- US Government Jobs.com   usgovernmentjobs.com
- Whitehouse   whitehouse.gov

The following popular federal government agencies also include employment information on their agency websites:

- African Development
  Foundation   www.adf.gov
- Agency for International
  Development (USAID)   www.usaid.gov
- Central Intelligence Agency www.cia.gov
- Consumer Product Safety
  Commission   www.cpsc.gov
- Department of Agriculture   www.usda.gov
- Department of Commerce   www.doc.gov
- Department of Defense   www.dtic.mil
- Department of Energy   www.energy.gov
- Department of Health
  and Human Services   www.os.dhhs.gov
- Department of Justice   www.usdoj.gov
- Department of State   www.state.gov
- Department of
  Transportation   www.dot.gov
- Environmental Protection
  Agency   www.epa.gov
- Export-Import Bank   www.exim.gov
- Federal Communications
  Commission   www.fcc.gov
- Federal Emergency
  Management Agency   www.fema.gov
- General Services
  Administration   www.gsa.gov

- Immigration and
  Naturalization Service   www.ins.usdoj.gov
- Inter-American Foundation   www.iaf.gov
- Internal Revenue Service   www.irs.ustreas.gov
- Peace Corps   www.peacecorps.com
- Smithsonian Institution   www.si.edu
- U.S. Postal Service   www.usps.gov

Nonprofit

Within the United States nearly 700,000 nonprofit organizations employ more than 10 million people. This employment sector offers numerous job opportunities for individuals oriented toward helping people or pursuing causes at home or abroad. While many nonprofits are charitable organizations involved in raising and dispensing funds, others promote policy agendas through education and lobbying efforts.

The following gateway sites provide quick access to both domestic and international nonprofit organizations:

- GuideStar   guidestar.org
- Action Without Borders   idealist.org
- Access   www.accessjobs.org

The following websites also function as gateway sites to the world of nonprofit organizations:

- Charity Village   charityvillage.com
- Council on Foundations   cof.org
- Foundation Center   fdncenter.org
- Impact Online   impactonline.org
- Independent Sector   indepsec.org
- Internet Nonprofit Center   nonprofits.org

International

While many international job seekers pursue careers in government and with nonprofit organizations, others are more oriented toward international business opportunities. The following websites are of special interest to international job seekers. Many of these sites include international job listings, resume databases, and linkages to other important international employment-related sites:

- EscapeArtist.com   escapeartist.com
- Monster.com   international.monster.com
- Overseas Jobs   overseasjobs.com
- JobsAbroad.com   jobsabroad.com
- Transitions Abroad   transitionsabroad.com
- iAgora.com   iagora.com

Several of the following international employment-related sites also should prove useful in conducting an international job search. Representing a wide range of job services – from high tech jobs and teaching English abroad to international headhunters and summer jobs – these sites are well worth visiting:

- About.com   intljobs.about.com
- AboutJobs.com   aboutjobs.com
- ActiJob.com   actijob.com
- Alliances Abroad   alliancesabroad.com
- CareerWeb   careerweb.com
- Dave's ESL Café   eslcafe.com
- Expat Exchange   www.expatexchange.com
- Global Career Center   globalcareercenter.com
- Heidrick & Struggles   heidrick.com
- International Jobs Center internationaljobs.org
- International Staffing
  Consultants   www.iscworld.com
- International Resources   umich.edu/~icenter/overseas/
  (key resource site)   work/workresources.html
- Job Monkey.com   jobmonkey.com
- Jobpilot.com   jobsadverts.com
- Jobshark.com   jobshark.com
- Jobs.Net   jobs.net
- JobsDB.com   jobsdb.com
- Jobware International   jobware.com
- Korn/Ferry International   ekornferry.com

- Nicholson International   nicholsonintl.com
- Management Recruiters
  International   brilliantpeople.com
- PlanetRecruit   planetrecruit.com
- PricewaterhouseCoopers   pwcglobal.com
- Spencer Stuart   spencerstuart.com
- Teaching Jobs Overseas   joyjobs.com
- Top Jobs   topjobs.net
- WorldWorkz   worldworkz.com

You'll also find hundreds of regional- and country-specific sites relevant to international job seekers. Monster.com alone operates 15 separate country sites through its "Global Network":

globalgateway.monster.com

For detailed information on these and other international employment sites, see *The Directory of Websites For International Jobs* (Impact Publications, 2002).

Part-Time, Temporary, and Contract

If you are joining the part-time, temporary, contract, and freelance workforce – those who are often referred to as "free agents" – you'll find numerous websites designed to link your interests and skills to employers in search of such flexible talent. A disproportionate number of these sites specialize in IT positions and offer everything from temporary project positions to full-time jobs. Some of the best such sites include:

- eLance   eLance.com
- BrainBid.com   brainbid.com
- eWork   ework.com

Numerous other websites offer services for a wide range of free agents who want to work part-time or as contract workers:

- A2Zmoonlighter.com   a2zmoonlighter.com
- Aquent Talent Finder   aquent.com
- Consultants-On-Demand   consultants-on-demand.com
- ContractJobHunter   cjhunter.com
- Contract-Jobs.com   contract-jobs.com
- Contractorforum.com   contractorforum.com
- Dice.com   dice.com
- Do a Project   doaproject.com
- ePlaced.com   eplaced.com
- FreeAgent.com   freeagent.com
- Guru.com   guru.com
- Handyman.com   handyman.com
- Icplanet   icplanet.com
- Itmoonlighter.com   itmoonlighter.com
- MBA Free Agents.com   www.mbaglobalnet.com/ freeagents.html
- Talentmarket.monster.com   talentmarket.monster.com
- Parttimejobstore.com   parttimejobstore.com
- Software Contractor's Guild   scguild.com
- Swiftwork   www.swiftwork.com
- TalentGateway   www.talentgateway.com
- Unicru   unicru.com

If you are primarily interested in working through a staffing agency, which may assign you to a variety of full-time and part-time positions, be sure to explore these major staffing firms. Most of them work with professionals:

- Staffing.com   staffing.com
- Net-Temps   net-temps.com
- Robert Half International   www.rhii.com
- Manpower   www.manpower.com
- Olsten Staffing Services   olsten.com
- Kelly Services   kellyservices.com

Freelancers and telecommuters also have their own set of websites that respond to their particular employment needs:

- All Freelance   allfreelance.com
- Bullhorn   bullhorn.com
- FreelanceJobSearch.com   freelancejobsearch.com
- FreelanceOnline.com   freelanceonline.com
- FreelanceWriting.com   freelancewriting.com
- Homeworking.com   homeworking.com
- Institute of Management
  Consultants   imcusa.org
- MediaStreet.com   mediastreet.com
- MoneyFromHome.com   moneyfromhome.com
- Nationwide Consultants   nationwideconsultants.com
- OutSource 2000   outsource2000.com
- Outsourcing Jobs   outsourcingjobs.com
- PortaJobs   portajobs.com
- Smarterwork.com   www.smarterwork.com
- Sologig.com   sologig.com
- Telecommuting Jobs   tjobs.com
- Telework Connection   telework-connection.com
- Womans-Work.com   womans-work.com
- Work at Home Moms   wahm.com
- WorkOnLine   telecommute.hypermart.net

As you will quickly discover, regardless of your occupational speciality, skills, or experience, there are numerous websites available to assist you in finding a job and managing your career. Indeed, there is a high level of redundancy among these sites. As such, they should help connect you to numerous employers who may be interested in your particular skills and experience.

12

Canadian Sites

I F YOU ARE CANADIAN OR IF YOU ARE INTERESTED IN
job opportunities in Canada, the websites featured in this chapter
will be of particular interest to you. While many of the U.S.-
based job board sites discussed in Chapter 7 and the international employment sites summarized in Chapter 11 include employment information relevant to Canada, the sites in this chapter are
primarily oriented toward the Canadian job market. Most are operated
by Canadian organizations that understand the nuances of the
Canadian job market. Many of these sites offer both English and
French language browsing options.

Top Employment Sites

Sparsely populated and geographically expansive, Canada is one of the
world's most highly wired countries with employment websites. Most
Canadian sites include job postings and resume databases. Some sites
also include useful career information and advice. Government at all
levels in Canada are very much involved in providing online employment information to the public. At the same time, several private

companies have organized employment websites similar to the many job sites operating in the United States.

The following sites represent some of the largest and most comprehensive employment websites in Canada. They include a great deal of career information and services in addition to the standard job postings and resume databases.

Workopolis.com **Mega Employment Site**
workopolis.com

This is one of Canada's largest and most comprehensive employment websites, which is affiliated with two major newspapers – *The Toronto Star* and *The Globe and Mail*. Well designed with numerous useful features, the site includes searchable job postings (30,000+ by job category, title, industry, and location), a resume database, and numerous online job search resources. The resource section includes career news, searchable articles, weekly tips, career advisors, industry research, success stories, education programs, surveys, and linkages to WorkNet and workplace columnist Bob Rosner.

Monster Canada **Mega Employment Site**
monster.ca

This is one of Monster.com's 15 international employment websites. Similar to other Monster.com sites, this one includes a resume database and job postings (more than 20,000) as well as a rich career resource section. The site includes a resume center, career articles and tips, forums, a practice interview center, interactive quizzes, a career horoscope, employer research center, and linkages to over 1 million international jobs. The site also includes an automatic email function which sends job seekers the latest job announcements. Like other Monster.com sites, this one includes an online poll.

Canjobs.com	Mega Job Board
canjobs.com	

Calling itself the "Canadian Employment Search Network," this employment website primarily offers searchable job postings and a resume database. Includes a quick search function to identify job listings by career type, province, and keyword. Also includes a network of separate websites for seven different provinces.

Numerous other Canadian employment websites include job postings, resume databases, email alert features, and job search tips. The following sites are primarily U.S.-based sites with Canadian sections or components

- **Careerbuilder.com**   careerbuilder.com
- **ContractJobHunter**   contractjobhunter.com
- **ExecuNet**   execunet.com
- **FlipDog Canada**   flipdog.com/js/cat.html?_
                                 requestid=923759
- **Headhunter.net Canada**   headhunter.net/JobSeeker/
                                 Jobs/jobfindica.asp
- **HotJobs Canada**   hotjobs.ca
- **JobSniper Canada**   jobsniper.com

The majority of Canadian employment websites are operated by Canadian companies or the Canadian government. The following list of websites represents some of the best we have found for employment purposes:

- **+ Jobs Canada**   plusjobs.ca
- **ActiJobs**   actijob.com
                                 canadajob.com
- **ActualJobs Canada**   actualjobs.com
- **All Canadian Jobs**   allcanadianjobs.com
- **Alumni-Network**   alumni-network.com

- AtlanticCanadaCareers — atlanticcanadacareers.com
- AtlanticJobs — atlanticjobs.com
- BrainsTalent — brainstalent.com
- Campus WorkLink — campusworklink.com
- Canada Career Consortium — careerccc.org
- Canada Job Centre — canadajobcentre.com
- Canada Job Search — canadajobsearch.com
- Canada Jobs — ijive.com
- CanadaIT.com — canadait.com
- Canadajobs.com — canadajobs.com
- Canadian Jobs — www.canadianjobs.com
- Canadian Careers.com — canadiancareers.com
- Canadian Employment Weekly — mediacorp2.com
- Canadian Jobs Catalog — www.kenevacorp.mb.ca
- Canadian Oil Field Jobs — jobs-canada.ca
- Canadian Public Service Jobs — jobs.gc.ca
- Canadian Resume Centre — canres.com
- Careerclick.com — careerclick.com
- Career Owl — careerowl.com
- Careers.org — careers.org
- CareerSite.com — careersite.com
- Charity Careers — charitycareers.com
- CharityVillage — charityvillage.com
- Job Bank Canada — jobbank.gc.ca
- Job Shark — jobshark.ca
- Jobs, Workers, and Careers — jobsetc.ca
- Newspaper Classifieds — workplace.hrdc-drhc.gc.ca/wantad.htm
- NetJobs.com — netjobs.com
- SkillNet.ca — skillnet.ca
- Yahoo! Canada (Jobs) — ca.yahoo.com

Career Information and Advice

While most employment websites focus on using job postings and resume databases, a few other sites primarily dispense online career information and advice. The following websites provide important research tools for job seekers who need to research industries, occupations, jobs, employers, and recruiters:

- Canada WorkinfoNet   workinfonet.ca
- Career Bookmarks   careerbookmarks.tpl.toronto.on.ca
- Career Development Manual   www.careerservices.uwaterloo.ca/manual-home.html
- Career/Lifeskills Resources   career-lifeskills.com
- Catapult   www.jobweb.com/catapult/home/canada.html
- Contact Point   contactpoint.ca
- Directory of Canadian Recruiters   directoryofrecruiters.com
- Job Futures 2000   jobfutures.ca
- WorkSearch   worksearch.gc.ca

Research Sites

Numerous websites provide invaluable information on jobs, industries, and employers in Canada. The following websites represent only a few of the many useful sites for conducting job search research:

- Advice for Investors   fin-info.com
- Canadian Corporate News: Annual Reports   ccn.ar.wilink.com/cgi-bin/start.pl
- Canadian Trade Index   ctidirectory.com
- Canadian Information Centre for International Credentials   cicic.ca
- CorporateInformation   corporateinformation.com/cacorp.html
- Newspapers/Magazines   www.newspapers.com
  canada.com/news
  onlinenewspapers.com/canada.htm
  newsdirectory.com/news/press/na/ca

- Research Company
  Information: Gateway   www.library.ubc.ca/lam/
  company_intro.html
- SEDAR: System for
  Electronic Document
  Analysis and Retrival   sedar.com
- Strategis: Business   strategis.ic.gc.ca/sc_indps/
  Information By Sector   engdoc/homepage.html
- Strategis: Canadian   strategis.ic.gc.ca/cgi-bin/sc_
  Company Capabilities   coinf/ccc/cccsrch?submit_
  srchscreen=basic&lang=
  e&search_screen=cc

- Strategis: Guide to   strategis.ic.gc.ca/sc_indps/
  Canadian Industries   gci/engdoc/homepage.html

Regional, Provincial, and Local Websites

Most regions, provinces, territories, and major cities have their own
employment websites. Some of these sites are part of the Canjobs.com
network. Depending on your geographic interests, the following sites
may prove useful:

Alberta

- Alberta Government
  Job Board   www.gov.ab.ca/pao/jobs
- AlbertaJobs   albertajobs.com

British Columbia

- BritishColumbiaJobs   britishcolumbiajobs.com
- British Columbia
  Goverment Jobs   postings.gov.bc.ca
- City of Vancouver Jobs   city.vancouver.bc.ca/human
  resources/jobs/jobspage.html

Manitoba

- Manitoba Civil Service   gov.mb.ca/csc/jobs

- ManitobaJobs.com   manitobajobs.com

New Brunswick

- Atlantic Canada   careerbeacon.com
- AtlanticJobs   atlanticjobs.com
- BrainsTalent   brainstalent.com
- NBJobNet   nbjobnet.gov.nb.ca

Newfoundland

- Atlantic Canada   careerbeacon.com
- AtlanticJobs   atlanticjobs.com
- BrainsTalent   brainstalent.com
- NewfoundlandCareers   newfoundlandcareers.com
- Newfoundland   www.gov.nf.ca/psc/
  Government Jobs   employment.htm
- NewfoundlandJobs   jobs.nf.ca
- NewfoundlandJobsite   newfoundlandjobsite.com

Northwest Territories

- Northwest Territories
  Government Jobs   www.gov.nt.ca/utility/jobs

Nova Scotia

- Atlantic Canada   careerbeacon.com
- AtlanticJobs   atlanticjobs.com
- BrainsTalent   brainstalent.com
- Jobs in Nova Scotia   jobsinnovascotia.com
- NovaScotiaJobShop   novascotiajobshop.ca

Ontario

- Go Jobs Ottawa   gojobs.gov.on.ca
- JobSearch.ca   jobsearch.ca
- JobSpotting.com (Ottawa)   jobspotting.com

- OntarioJobs.com   ontariojobs.com
- OttawaJob.com   ottawajob.com

Prince Edward Island

- Atlantic Canada   careerbeacon.com
- AtlanticJobs   atlanticjobs.com
- BrainsTalent   brainstalent.com
- Prince Edward Island
  Government Jobs   www.gov.pe.ca/jobs

Quebec

- QuebecJobs   quebecjobs.com
- QuebecJobSite   quebecjobsite.com

Saskatchewan

- Saskatchewan
  Government Jobs   www.gov.sk.ca/psc/jobs
- Saskjobs.com   saskjobs.com

Tip of the Iceberg

Clients of Bernard Haldane Associates have access, through its proprietary CS2K program, to a huge database of Canadian websites. These sites enable job seekers to quickly explore job listings, enter their resume into a database, research employers, and acquire useful job search information and advice. The sites identified in this chapter will help you get started on your own Canadian job search.

13

United Kingdom Sites

I F YOUR JOB AND CAREER INTERESTS FOCUS ON EM-
ployers in the United Kingdom, you should definitely incorporate
the Internet in your job search. Numerous international and UK-
specific employment websites provide a wealth of job search
information and services, from job postings and resume databases to
employment research and job search advice. Many of these sites also
incorporate Ireland and several cities on the Continent. Similar to job
seekers in the United States and Canada, you can use the Internet to
quickly gain access to thousands of job listings throughout the United
Kingdom, enter your resume or CV into numerous online databases,
and apply for jobs online, and use several online job search resources
for sharpening your job search.

Gateway Employment Sites

While most employment websites in the United Kingdom are primarily job posting and CV database sites, a few function as useful
gateway sites to job boards and related employment websites. Be sure
to initially include these gateway sites in your job search:

Jobs UK	Gateway Site
jobs.co.uk	

This is the UK's premier gateway site to online job boards. It includes a "Quick Search" section for finding job boards by 30 occupational fields and 12 regional locations. It also includes a useful career resources section with information on writing a CV, interviewing, finding job discussion boards, linking to industries, locating salary data, and much more. Features the top 10 job boards. A very useful site for navigating through more than 500 UK job boards.

Ciao	Gateway/Evaluation Site
uk.ciao.com	

This site offers consumer reviews of numerous websites. Click on to the "Education and Careers" section which will take you to a list of the eight top employment ("recruitment agencies") sites. Consumers evaluate each site in terms of its database and search facilities, navigation, validity of job postings, frequency of content update, and ease of registration.

Three other websites also function as gateways to the world of employment sites in the United Kingdom:

- **Redundancy Help**   redundancyhelp.co.uk
- **Good Shop Guide**   thegoodshopguide.com/
                                                jobs.html
- **AIRSdirectory**   airsdirectory.com/jobboards

Top Employment Sites

Similar to U.S. and Canadian employment websites, numerous public and private organizations in the United Kingdom provide online employment information and services. Several U.S.-based mega employment websites outlined in Chapter 5, such as careerbuilder.com and flipdog.com, include sections on the United Kingdom.

Several of the largest and most popular employment websites in the United Kingdom include:

Total Jobs	**Mega Employment Site**
totaljobs.com	

This site includes over 40,000 searchable job postings by occupational category, location, and keywords. It also allows job seekers to enter their CV online, research companies, review salary information, and assess their career health (site generates a free 8-page assessment report for users). Includes a career news section.

Workthing	**Mega Employment Site**
workthing.com	

This popular site includes thousands of searchable job postings covering numerous job sectors. Offers a wealth of job search advice on everything from writing a winning CV to attracting a headhunter and negotiating salary. Job seekers can enter their CVs online and have new job announcements emailed directly to them. One of the few employment sites to offer unique content for numerous job sectors.

Jobpilot	**Mega Employment Site**
jobpilot.co.uk	

This user-friendly site offers one of the largest and most comprehensive collections of information and services to job seekers. Includes nearly 100,000 job postings, CV database, company profiles, and a "Career Journal" that includes CV tips, interview tips, negotiation strategies, resignation tips, and salary surveys. Includes special career channels for international job seekers, HR professionals, students, and legal issues. Also includes career news and information for foreigners wishing to work in the UK – work permits, visas, employment contracts, holidays, salaries, working hours, and how to get started.

Monster UK   Mega Employment Site
monster.co.uk

Similar to Monster sites found in 14 other countries, this site is huge and comprehensive. Includes more than 30,000 job postings in its searchable database. Job seekers can create an online CV and upload it to the site's CV database. They also can have new job postings automatically emailed to them. The site is rich with job search information and tips, such as how to write a CV and prepare for a job interview, which are included in a "Career Centre." Includes featured employers, communities, relocation tips, and links to Monster's network of separate country sites.

Gojobsite   Mega Employment Site
gojobsite.com

This site is largely oriented to the UK and European job market with its nearly 300,000 advertised job openings each month. Covers France, Germany, Ireland, Italy, Spain, and the United Kingdom (jobsite.co.uk). Includes a searchable database of nearly 40,000 job postings for 35 industry sectors, career news, job search advice, and more. Job seekers can elect to have new postings automatically emailed to them.

Fish4Jobs   Mega Employment Site
fish4jobs.com

This well designed site allows job seekers to search more than 40,000 job postings by title and location. Individuals also can explore different career paths which include information on responsibilities and duties, salaries, breaking in, training and qualifications, industry organizations, trade publications, and job listings. Also includes job-finding advice, recruiter profiles, and company information.

Gis-a-Job!	Mega Employment Site
gisajob.com	

This well designed and flashy site allows job seekers to search for thousands of job listings by sector, location, type, and keyword. Job seekers also can enter and update their CV online, research jobs and agencies, explore top employment websites, survey news, receive job postings by email, and explore job search resources, such as how to improve one's CV and prepare for an interview.

Milkround	Mega Employment Site
www.milkround.com	

Designed for graduate recruitment, this site includes numerous online employment opportunities with leading UK recruiters, job search advice, and employment news. Individuals can create their own online profile, apply online for jobs, receive job posting announcements and news by email, and complete an online personality assessment (Milkround Personality Questionnaire). This website also includes a "Learning City" which is powered by Wide Learning.

Numerous other employment websites provide a wealth of job search information, advice, and services. As with the previously featured sites, most of the following websites are primarily job boards with thousands of job listings and CV databases. Some sites specialize in a few occupational specialties.

- +Jobs UK — uk.plusjobs.com
- 1st Class Jobs — 1stjob.co.uk
- 3sectorsjobs — 3sectorsjob.com
- AgencyCentral — agencycentral.co.uk
- BigBlueDog — bigbluedog.com
- Brookstreet — www.brookstreet.co.uk
- Businessfile — businessfile-online.com
- CareerGlobe — careerglobe.co.uk
- City Jobs (UK & Europe) — cityjobs.com
- Contractor UK — contractoruk.co.uk
- CV-Library — www.cv-library.co.uk
- CVPoster.com — cvposter.com
- Cyber-CV.com — www.cyber-cv.com
- Cyberia — cyberiacafe.net
- E-job — e-job.net
- Education-Jobs — www.education-jobs.co.uk
- Employment Service — employmentservice.gov.uk
- First Division Jobs — www.firstdivisionjobs.com
- First-DivisionPeople — www.first-divisionpeople.uk.com
- First4London Jobs — first4london.com/jobs
- FTCareerPoint — ftcareerpoint.ft.com/ftcareerpoint
- Goldensquare — goldensquare.com
- Gradunet — www.gradunet.co.uk
- Guardian Unlimited — jobs.guardian.co.uk
- Homeworking.com — homeworking.com
- Qworx — qworx.com
- IT Job Bank — it-jobbank.co.uk
- Job Channel — job-channel.com
- Job Island — uk.jobisland.com
- JobMagic.net — jobmagic.net
- Jobs-At — www.jobs-at.co.uk
- Jobserve — www.jobserve.co.uk
- Job Shark — www.jobshark.co.uk
- JobSniper UK — jobsniper.com
- JobTrack — jobtrack.co.uk
- Jobzone — jobzoneuk.co.uk

- London Careers   londoncareers.net
- London Jobs Guide   www.londonjobsguide.co.uk
- Manpower   www.manpoweronline.net
- NetJobs   www.netjobs.co.uk
- New Monday   newmonday.com
- PeopleBank   peoplebank.com
- Personnel Store   personnelstore.com
- PhDjobs   phdjobs.com
- PlanetRecruit   planetrecruit.com/channel/uk
- Prospects   prospects.ac.uk
- Public Sector Jobs   jobs4publicsector.com
- QuantumJobs   www.quantumjobs.com
- Recruit-Online   www.recruit-online.co.uk
- Reed   www.reed.co.uk
- Secretaries   secsinthecity.com
- Stepstone   stepstone.co.uk
- TechJobs.co.uk   www.techjobs.co.uk
- Topjobs   topjobs.co.uk
- Total Jobs   totaljobs.com
- Travel Industry Jobs   www.travelindustryjobs.co.uk
- UK Contract Search   contract-search.com
- UK Jobs   ukjobs.com
- WorkTrain   worktrain.gov.uk
- Yahoo!   uk.yahoo.com

Career Information and Advice

A few employment-related sites primarily dispense job information and advice. The following sites are well worth visiting for tips on how to conduct an effective job search. They include numerous articles and expert advice on a wide range of employment subjects:

- Alec's Free CV, Job Hunting
  and Interview Tips   alec.co.uk
- Catapult   www.jobweb.com/catapult/
  home/uk.html
- Drjob.co.uk   drjob.co.uk
- Insidecareers   www.insidecareers.co.uk

- LineOne   www.lineone.net/business/
                         jobs
- Pathfinder-One   www.pathfinder-one.com

Research Sites

Conducting research on companies, employers, and communities is essential to any job search. Consider including many of these websites in your research plan:

- 192 Enquiries   192enquiries.com
- Bird-online   bird-online.co.uk
- British Companies   www.britishcompanies.co.uk
- Business Guide   guide-u.co.uk/business
- Carol Annual Reports   carol.co.uk
- CorporateInformation   corporateinformation.com/
                         ukcorp.html
- Corporate Reports   www.corpreports.co.uk
- Hoover's UK   hoovers.com/uk
- London Stock Exchange londonstockexchange.com
- NewsNow   newsnow.co.uk
- Newspapers/Magazines   onlinenewspapers.com/
                           england.htm
                         newsdirectory.com
                         www.newspapers.com
- NISS (National Information
  Services and Systems) www.niss.ac.uk
- Occupational Information www.prospects.csu.ac.uk/
                         student/cidd/occupat.htm
- The Times   www.thetimes.co.uk

The Haldane Database

As in the case of Canada and the United States, the Haldane proprietary CS2K program includes an expansive database of UK websites for assisting clients with their online job search activities targeted on the UK job market. The sites featured in this chapter represent only a few of the many websites which continue to define the United

Kingdom's ever expanding online job market. Incorporating many of these websites in your job search should save you a great deal of time in connecting with the right job.

APPENDIX

Bernard Haldane
Associates Network

MANY SELF-DIRECTED CAREER BOOKS CAN HELP you become more effective with your job search. They outline useful principles, suggest effective strategies, and explain how you and others can achieve your own job and career success. That's our purpose in writing this and other books in the "Haldane's Best" series. We believe you can benefit greatly from the methods we have developed over the years and have used successfully with hundreds of thousands of our clients.

We know the Haldane methods work because our clients are real cases of success that go far beyond the anecdotal. Indeed, our files are filled with unsolicited testimonials from former clients who have shared their insights into what really worked – evidence of our effectiveness in delivering what we promise our clients. We've shared some of these testimonials in this book. What especially pleases us as career professionals is the fact that we've helped change the lives of so many people who have gone on to renewed career success. They discovered new opportunities that were a perfect fit for their particular interests, skills, and abilities. By focusing on their strengths and identifying their motivated skills and abilities, they were able to chart new and exciting career directions.

But our clients didn't achieve success overnight nor on their own. They worked with a structure, a schedule, and a vision of what they wanted to do next with their lives. Most important of all, they worked with a Career Advisor who helped them every step of the way. What we and other career professionals have learned over the years is no real secret, but it's worth repeating:

> Most job seekers can benefit tremendously by working with a trained and experienced career professional who helps them complete each step of the career management process.

Client Feedback

"You cannot ask questions of a book. You cannot get feedback on what to do from a book. And most of all, no book can help you with a job hunting campaign designed specifically for you. This is where Haldane comes in."

– J.A.C.

Our methods are not quick and easy, nor do they come naturally to most people – especially if you want to make the right career move. Many of our clients come to us after several weeks and months of frustrated efforts in conducting their own job search. Some tried doing everything according to the books, but they soon discovered that the books are only as good as the actions and outcomes that follow. What they most needed, and later appreciated, was a career professional whom they could work with in completing the critical assessment work (Success Factor Analysis) and in relating that key data to all other stages in their job search, from resume and letter writing to networking and interviewing. Using the proprietary Career Strategy 2000 electronic system, they gained access to a huge database of opportunities and employers. Once our clients decide to "do it the Haldane way" with a Career Advisor, they get surprising results. Again and again their testimonials emphasize the importance of completing Success Factor Analysis, developing a Haldane objective, networking, writing focused resumes and "T" letters, and interviewing and negotiating salary according to Haldane principles. Most important of all, they point out the value of having someone there – a Haldane Career Advisor – to guide them through the psychological ups and downs that often come with the highly ego-involved and rejection-ridden job finding process.

There's a season for everything, be it reading a self-directed career book or contacting a career professional for assistance. We've shared with you our insights and strategies by writing this book. Now it's up to you to take the next step. What you do next may make a critical difference in your career and your life. You may well discover your dream job on your own because you organized a Haldane-principled job search. If and when you feel you could benefit from the assistance of a career professional, please consider the Haldane network of Career Advisors. They have an exceptional track record of success based upon the methods outlined in this and other books in the "Haldane's Best" series. For your convenience, we've listed, along with contact information, the more than 90 offices that make up the Haldane network in the United States, Canada, and the United Kingdom. You can contact the office nearest you for more information and arrange for a free consultation. Please visit our website for additional information on Bernard Haldane Associates:

www.jobhunting.com

United States

ALABAMA

10 Inverness Parkway, Suite 125
Birmingham, AL 35242
Tel. 205-991-9134
Fax 205-991-7164
bhaldane@careerleader.net

303 Williams Avenue, Suite 128
Huntsville, AL 35801
Tel. 256-512-5559
Fax 256-512-5564
Bhahts@aol.com

ARIZONA

3101 N. Central Ave., Suite 1560
Phoenix, AZ 85012
Tel. 602-248-8893
Fax 602-248-8987
BHAphoenix@digizip.com

5151 E. Broadway, Suite 750
Tucson, AZ 85711
Tel. 520-790-2767
Fax 520-790-2992
Tucson@bernardhaldane.com

ARKANSAS

10825 Financial Center Parkway
Suite 321
Little Rock, AR 72211
Tel. 501-907-7170
Fax 501-907-7174
LRHaldane2@alltel.net

CALIFORNIA

1801 Avenue of the Stars
Suite 1011
Los Angeles, CA 90067
Tel. 310-203-0955
Fax 310-203-0933
Labha@careers.com

101 Golf Course Drive, Suite 210
Rohnert Park, CA 94928
Tel. 707-585-8060
Fax 707-939-3764
Bhawc@flashcom.net

8801 Folsom Boulevard, Suite 100
Sacramento, CA 95826
Tel. 916-381-5094
Fax 916-381-6506
Bhasac@aol.com

8880 Rio San Diego Drive
Suite 300
San Diego, CA 92108
Tel. 619-299-1424
Fax 619-299-5340
Sandiego@bernardhaldane.com

233 Sansome Street, Suite 1111
San Francisco, CA 94104
Tel. 415-391-8087
Fax 415-391-4009
Haldane@job-hunting.com

181 Metro Drive, Suite 410
San Jose, CA 95110-1346
Tel. 408-437-9200
Fax 408-437-1300
Haldane@job-hunting.com

Pacific Plaza
1340 Treat Boulevard, Suite 220
Walnut Creek, CA 94596
Tel. 925-945-0776
Fax 925-939-3764
Bhawc@flashcom.net

COLORADO

Plaza of the Rockies
111 S. Tejon Street, Suite 610
Colorado Springs,
   CO 80903-2263
Tel. 719-634-8000
Fax 719-635-8008
Springs@haldane.com

1625 Broadway, #2550
Denver, CO 80202
Tel. 303-825-5700
Fax 303-825-5900
Denver@haldane.com

6053 S. Quebec Street
Suite 203
Englewood, CO 80111
Tel. 303-825-5700
Fax 303-265-9419
Denver@haldane.com

1075 W. Horsetooth Road
Suite 204
Fort Collins, CO 80526
Tel. 970-223-9300
Fax 970-223-9308
Poudre@haldane.com

CONNECTICUT

State House Square
Six Central Row
Hartford, CT 06103-2701
Tel. 860-247-7500
Fax 860-247-1213
Hartford@haldane.com

FLORIDA

Plantation Center
8201 West Peters Road
Suite 1000
Plantation, FL 33324
(Ft. Lauderdale)
Tel. 954-916-2777
Fax 954-916-2799
Jobs@bhaldane.com

6622 Southpoint Drive South
Suite 340
Jacksonville, FL 32216
Tel. 904-296-6802
Fax 904-296-3506
jacksonville@bernardhaldane.com

Brickell Center
1221 Brickell Center, Suite 900
Miami, FL 33131
Tel. 305-377-8740
Fax 305-377-8741
Jobs@bhaldane.com

901 North Lake Destiny Drive
Suite 379
Maitland, FL 32751
(Orlando)
Tel. 407-660-8323
Fax 407-660-2434
orlando@bernardhaldane.com

5100 W. Kennedy Boulevard
Suite 425
Tampa, FL 33609
Tel. 813-287-1393
Fax 813-289-4125
tampa@bernardhaldane.com

GEORGIA

4360 Chamblee Dunwoody Road
Suite 100
Atlanta, GA 30341
Tel. 770-455-1244
Fax 770-455-1266
Haldane@mindspring.com

ILLINOIS

One Magnificent Mile
980 N. Michigan Avenue
Suite 1400
Chicago, IL 60611
Tel. 312-214-4920
Fax 312-214-7674
Jobs@bhaldane.com

One Tower Lane
Suite 1700
Oakbrook Terrace, IL 60181
Tel. 630-573-2923
Fax 630-574-7048
Jobs@bhaldane.com

1901 N. Roselle Road
Suite 800
Schaumburg, IL 60195
Tel. 847-490-6454
Fax 847-490-6529
Jobs@bhaldane.com

INDIANA

8888 Keystone Crossing,
Suite 1675
Indianapolis, IN 46240
Tel. 317-846-6062
Fax 317-846-6354
BHA_Indy_Admn@worldnet.att.net

105 E. Jefferson Blvd.
Suite 800
South Bend, IN 46601
Tel. 219-246-8682
Fax 219-246-8683
Jobs@bhaldane.com

IOWA

6165 NW 86th Street
Johnston, IA 50131
(Des Moines)
Tel. 515-727-1623
Fax 515-727-1673
HaldaneIowa@aol.com

KANSAS

7007 College Boulevard
Suite 727
Overland Park, KS 66211
Tel. 913-327-0300
Fax 913-327-7067
resume@kchaldane.com

2024 N. Woodlawn
Suite 402
Wichita, KS 67208
Tel. 316-687-5333
Fax 316-689-6924
sendresume@wkhaldane.com

KENTUCKY

330 E. Main Street, Suite 200
Lexington, KY 40507
Tel. 859-255-2163
Fax 859-231-0737
BHA_Lex_Admn@worldnet.att.net

9100 Shelbyville Road
Suite 280
Louisville, KY 40222
Tel. 502-326-5121
Fax 502-426-5348
BHA_Louis_Admn@worldnet.att.net

MAINE

477 Congress Street
5th Floor
Portland, ME 04101-3406
Tel. 207-772-1700
Fax 207-772-7117
Jobhunting@haldane.com

MASSACHUSETTS

277 Dartmouth Street
Corner of Newbury Street
Boston, MA 02116-2800
Tel. 617-247-2500
Fax 617-247-7171
Jobhunting@haldane.com

MICHIGAN

5777 West Maple Road
Suite 190
West Bloomfield, MI 48322
(Detroit)
Tel. 248-737-4700
Fax 248-737-4789
Bhadet@ameritech.net

MINNESOTA

3433 Broadway Street, NE
Suite 150
Minneapolis, MN 55413
Tel. 612-378-0600
Fax 612-378-9225
Jobs@bhaldane.com

MISSOURI

680 Craig Road, Suite 400
St. Louis, MO 63141
Tel. 314-991-5444
Fax 314-991-5207
Careers@haldanestl.com

NEBRASKA

12020 Shamrock Plaza, Suite 200
Omaha, NE 68154
Tel. 402-330-9461
Tel. 402-330-9847
Omaha@haldanestl.com

NEVADA

8275 S. Eastern Ave., Suite 200
Las Vegas, NV 89123
Tel. 702-990-8540
Fax 702-938-1050
Bhavegas@hotmail.com

NEW JERSEY

100 Princeton Overlook Center
Suite 100
Princeton, NJ 08540
Tel. 609-987-0400
Fax 609-987-0011
Jobs@bhaldane.com

101 Eisenhower Pkwy., Suite 300
Roseland, NJ 07068
Tel. 973-795-1202
Fax 973-795-1278
Jobs@bhaldane.com

NEW YORK

80 State Street, 11th Floor
Albany, NY 12207
Tel. 518-447-1000
Fax 518-447-0011
Jobhunting@haldane.com

300 International Drive, Suite 213
Williamsville, NY 14221
(Buffalo)
Tel. 716-626-3400
Fax 716-626-3402
Jobhunting@haldane.com

50 Charles Lindbergh Boulevard
Suite 400
Uniondale, NY 11553
(Long Island)
Tel. 516-390-4780
Fax 516-390-4781
Jobs@bhaldane.com

261 Madison Avenue, Suite 1504
New York, NY 10016
Tel. 212-490-7799
Fax 212-490-1712
Jobs@bhaldane.com

838 Crosskeys Office Park
Fairport, NY 14450
(Rochester)
Tel. 716-425-0550
Fax 716-425-0554
Haldane@frontiernet.net

5000 Campuswood Drive
East Syracuse, NY 13057
(Syracuse)
Tel. 315-234-5627
Fax 315-234-5628
Haldane@frontiernet.net

520 White Plains Road
Suite 500
Tarrytown, NY 10591
Tel. 914-467-7818
Fax 914-467-7817
Jobs@bhaldane.com

NORTH CAROLINA

6100 Fairview Road, Suite 355
Charlotte, NC 28210
Tel. 704-643-5959
Fax 704-556-1674
Charlotte@haldanestl.com

4011 West Chase Boulevard
Suite 210
Raleigh, NC 27607
Tel. 919-546-9759
Fax 919-546-9766
Raleigh@haldanestl.com

OHIO

3250 W. Market Street, Suite 101
Akron, OH 44333
Tel. 330-867-7889
Fax 330-867-7874
GCMG_HQ@worldnet.att.net

625 Eden Park Dr., Suite 775
Cincinnati, OH 45202
Tel. 513-621-4440
Fax 513-562-8943
BHA_Cincy_Admn@worldnet.att.net

6000 Lombardo Center
Suite 150
Independence, OH 44131
(Cleveland)
Tel. 216-447-0166
Fax 216-447-0015
BHA_Clev_Admn@worldnet.att.net

111 West Rich Street, Suite 480
Columbus, OH 43215
Tel. 614-224-2322
Fax 614-224-2333
BHA_Colb_Admn@worldnet.att.net

Fifth Third Center
110 N. Main Street, Suite 1280
Dayton, OH 45402
Tel. 937-224-5279
Fax 937-224-5284
*BHA_Dayton_Admn@worldnet.
att.net*

3131 Executive Parkway
Suite 106
Toledo, OH 43606
Tel. 419-535-3898
Fax 419-531-4771
Bhadet@ameritech.net

OKLAHOMA

3030 NW Expressway
Suite 727
Oklahoma City, OK 73112
Tel. 405-948-7668
Fax 405-948-7869
Bhaokc@coxinet.net

7060 South Yale, Suite 707
Tulsa, OK 74136
Tel. 918-491-9151
Fax 918-491-9153
Bhatulsa@swbell.net

OREGON

1220 S.W. Morrison
Suite 800
Portland, OR 97205
Tel. 503-295-5926
Fax 503-295-2639
Portland@bernardhaldane.com

PENNSYLVANIA

Parkview Tower
1150 First Avenue, Suite 385
King of Prussia, PA 19406
(Philadelphia)
Tel. 610-491-9050
Fax 610-491-9080
Jobs@bhaldane.com

Three Gateway Center, 18 East
401 Liberty Avenue
Pittsburgh, PA 15222
Tel. 412-263-5627
Fax 412-263-2027
Bhapittspa@aol.com

<u>*RHODE ISLAND*</u>

1400 BankBoston Plaza
Providence, RI 02903
Tel. 401-272-6400
Fax 401-272-6446
Providence@haldane.com

<u>*SOUTH CAROLINA*</u>

3800 Fernandina Rd., Suite 260
Columbia, SC 29210
Tel. 803-750-9155
Fax 803-772-9163
Columbia@haldanestl.com

<u>*TENNESSEE*</u>

735 Broad Street, Suite 802
Chattanooga, TN 37402
Tel. 423-265-6100
Fax 423-265-6102
Chattanooga@haldaneonline.com

7610 Gleason Drive, Suite 301
Knoxville, TN 37919
Tel. 865-690-6767
Fax 865-690-3990
BHAknoxadmin@worldnet.att.net

3150 Lenox Park Blvd, Suite 302
Memphis, TN 38115
Tel. 901-375-1111
Fax 901-375-1545
Memphis@haldanestl.com

424 Church Street, Suite 1625
Nashville, TN 37219
Tel. 615-742-8440
Fax 615-742-8445
Jobs@bhaldane.com

<u>*TEXAS*</u>

98 San Jacinto Blvd., Suite 300
Austin, TX 78701
Tel. 512-867-3535
Fax 512-867-3537
Austin@bernardhaldane.com

Park Central VII
12750 Merit Drive, Suite 200
Dallas, TX 75251
Tel. 972-503-4100
Fax 972-503-4445
Dallas@bernardhaldane.com

1300 Post Oak Boulevard
Suite 950
Houston, TX 77056
Tel. 713-622-5151
Fax 713-622-6161
Houston@bernardhaldane.com

<u>*UTAH*</u>

215 South State Street
Suite 200
Salt Lake City, UT 84111
Tel. 801-355-4242
Fax 801-355-3238
bhajobs@slchaldane.com

<u>*VIRGINIA*</u>

2101 Wilson Boulevard
Suite 950
Arlington, VA 22201
Tel. 703-516-9122
Fax 703-812-3001
Jobs@bhaldane.com

6800 Paragon Place
Suite 106
Richmond, VA 23230
Tel. 804-282-0470
Fax 804-282-1983
Jobs@bhaldane.com

<u>*WASHINGTON*</u>

10900 N.E. 8th Street
Suite 1122
Bellevue, WA 98004
(Seattle)
Tel. 425-462-7308
Fax 425-462-9670
CareersPNW@aol.com

West 818 Riverside Avenue
Suite 320
Spokane, WA 99201
Tel. 509-325-7650
Fax 509-325-7655
CareersSPO@aol.com

917 Pacific Avenue, Suite 400
Tacoma, WA 98402
Tel. 253-383-8757
Fax 253-383-0887
CareersADV@aol.com

WISCONSIN

4351 W. College Ave., Suite 215
Appleton, WI 54914
Tel. 920-831-7820
Fax 920-831-7831
Appleton@bhawi.com

5315 Wall Street, Suite 200
Madison, WI 53718
Tel. 608-246-2100
Fax 608-246-2031
Madison@bhawi.com

15800 W. Bluemound Road
Suite 320
Brookfield, WI 53005
(Milwaukee)
Tel. 262-797-9971
Fax 262-797-9002
Milwaukee@bhawi.com

CANADA

ALBERTA

Bow Valley Square III
255 – 5th Avenue SW
Suite 710, 7th Floor
Calgary, AB   T2P 3G6
Tel. 403-265-1372
Fax 403-265-1382
Careers@bhawest.com

Manulife Place
Executive Centre, Suite 1000
10180 - 101 Street
Edmonton, AB   T5J 3S4
Tel. 780-423-2090
Fax 780-423-2097
Careersedmonton@bhawest.com

BRITISH COLUMBIA

IBM Tower
701 West Georgia St., Suite 1800
Vancouver, BC   V7Y 1C6
Tel. 604-609-6661
Fax 604-609-2638
Careers@bhawest.com

ONTARIO

3027 Harvester Road
Suite 105
Burlington, ONT   L7N 3G7
Tel. 905-681-0180
Fax 905-681-0181
Careers@bhaburl.com

255 Queens Avenue
Suite 2150
London, ONT   N6A 5R8
Tel. 519-439-2580
Fax 519-439-2587
Bhaldane@netcom.ca

55 Metcalfe Street
Suite 1460
Ottawa, ONT   K1P 6L5
Tel. 613-234-2530
Fax 613-234-2560
Bhaottawa@aol.com

350 Bay Street
9th Floor
Toronto, ONT   M5H 2S6
Tel. 416-363-9241
Fax 416-363-9246
BHAToronto@aol.com

1250 Blvd. Rene-Levesque Ouest
Suite 2335
Montreal, QUE H3B 4W8
Tel. 514-938-0578
Fax 514-938-9165
Bhaldane@bha.attcanada.net

MANCHESTER

Portland Tower
Portland Street
Manchester M1 3LF
Tel. 011-44-1612-384946
Fax 011-44-1612-384918
manchester@bernardhaldane.co.uk

United Kingdom

BIRMINGHAM

43 Temple Row
Birmingham B2 5LS
Tel. 011-44-1212-376015
Fax 011-44-1212-376121
birmingham@bernardhaldane.co.uk

BRISTOL

First Floor, Aztec Centre
Aztec West
Almondsbury
Bristol BS32 4TD
Tel. 011-44-1454-203700
Fax 011-44-1454-203701
Bristol@bernardhaldane.co.uk

LEEDS

1 City Square
Leeds LS1 2ES
Tel. 011-44-1133-002031
Fax 011-44-1133-002638
leeds@bernardhaldane.co.uk

LONDON

Marcol House
289/293 Regent Street
London W1B 2HJ
Tel. 011-44-2072-909100
Fax 011-44-2072-909109
London@bernardhaldane.co.uk

Index

Haldane's Best

The following Haldane titles are available in bookstores or can be ordered directly from the publisher:

IMPACT PUBLICATIONS
9104 Manassas Drive, Suite N
Manassas Park, VA 20111-5211
1-800-361-1055 (orders only)
Tel. 703-361-7300 or Fax 703-335-9486
Email address: *info@impactpublications.com*
Quick and Easy online ordering: *www.impactpublications.com*

Orders from individuals must be prepaid by check, money order, Visa, Mastercard, or American Express. We accept telephone and fax orders.

Qty.	Titles	Price	Total
____	Haldane's Best Answers to Tough Interview Questions	$15.95	_____
____	Haldane's Best Cover Letters for Professionals	15.95	_____
____	Haldane's Best Employment Websites for Professionals	15.95	_____
____	Haldane's Best Resumes for Professionals	15.95	_____
____	Haldane's Best Salary Tips for Professionals	15.95	_____

SUBTOTAL _____

Virginia residents add 4 ½% sales tax . . . . _____

POSTAGE/HANDLING ($5 for first product and 8% of SUBTOTAL over $30) $5.00

8% of SUBTOTAL over $30 . . . . _____

TOTAL ENCLOSED . . . . _____

NAME _____

ADDRESS _____

_____

_____

Credit Card Orders: Please include credit card number, expiration date, and signature.